I0114131

BURNED BY BILLION-AIRES

OTHER BOOKS BY CHUCK COLLINS

Economic Apartheid in America
(with Felice Yeskel)

Wealth and Our Commonwealth
(with Bill Gates Sr.)

Moral Measure of the Economy
(with Mary Wright)

Born on Third Base

Is Inequality in America Irreversible?

The Wealth Hoarders

Altar to an Erupting Sun

BURNED BY BILLION-AIRES

How Concentrated Wealth and Power Are Ruining Our Lives and Planet

CHUCK COLLINS

NEW YORK
LONDON

Published in the United States by The New Press, New York, 2025
Distributed by Two Rivers Distribution

ISBN 978-1-62097-909-9 (hc)
ISBN 978-1-62097-996-9 (ebook)
CIP data is available

The New Press publishes books that promote and enrich public discussion and understanding of the issues vital to our democracy and to a more equitable world. These books are made pos si ble by the enthusiasm of our readers; the support of a committed group of donors, large and small; the collaboration of our many partners in the independent media and the not-for-profit sector; booksellers, who often hand-sell New Press books; librarians; and above all by our authors.

www.thenewpress.org

Book design and composition by Brian Mulligan
This book was set in Sabon MT

Printed in the United States of America

To Sam Pizzigati
Colleague, Scholar, Mentor

CONTENTS

BURNED BY BILLION-AIRES

INTRODUCTION

TAKE IT PERSONALLY

*I wanna be a billionaire so f**king bad*
Buy all of the things I never had
I wanna be on the cover of Forbes magazine
Smiling next to Oprah and the Queen

—Travie McCoy, "Billionaire"

ONE HUNDRED AND FORTY YEARS AGO, AMERICAN INDUSTRIALIZATION gave rise to an unprecedented aggregation of wealth among a small number of businessmen. A handful of them—most famously John D. Rockefeller, Andrew Carnegie, and Cornelius Vanderbilt—amassed fortunes by cornering the market in oil, steel, and railroad construction, earning them the moniker "robber barons." In his satiric novel of the same name, Mark Twain would dub this era "the Gilded Age" (roughly 1880–1915) to refer to the greed, graft, and corruption that lay beneath its glittering facade. These industrialists' outsize wealth and power over the lives of ordinary Americans eventually fueled a popular movement of workers and farmers that successfully pushed for business regulations and labor protections in the early twentieth century.

We are now in the midst of a Second Gilded Age, one that has surpassed the first in its degree of wealth accumulation and inequality.

Between 1983 and 2024, the number of billionaires in the United States increased more than fiftyfold—from fifteen to more than eight hundred.[1] The number of multi-millionaire households—those worth between $10 million and $100 million—has jumped tenfold. You might read these figures and think, "Well, I guess that's proof that the American economy is doing really well; and more power to them, because I sure would like to be that rich one day!" Or maybe you feel deep gratitude for Amazon same-day delivery, and for the technological wonders of Starlink, Facebook, and Chat GPT, and accordingly you aren't inclined to begrudge Jeff Bezos, Elon Musk, or Mark Zuckerberg their billions. After all, shouldn't American innovation be richly rewarded?

Or perhaps you vacillate between envy, appreciation, and a slightly queasy feeling that something about how billionaires are faring versus the rest of us is not quite right. We know from polling data that increasing numbers of Americans—seven in ten Americans in a 2024 poll—now believe that "wealth inequality is a serious national issue."[2]

Burned by Billionaires is about the impact that the ultra-wealthy—the tippy-top .01 percent—have on the lives of the rest of us and on our well-being as a society. As the title suggests, I argue that their collective impact is a serious cause for concern. What this book is *not* is a critique of the behavior of individual billionaires.

To be sure, there are abundant examples of billionaires behaving badly, and having an enormous amount of wealth amplifies exponentially the impact of a single person's greed or antisocial behavior. We might not care that Elon Musk has a juvenile sense of humor, were it not for the fact that he purchased one of the world's largest social media platforms, where he now broadcasts disinformation and conspiracy theories that are actively undermining democracy; or that he has essentially bought himself an unelected vice presidency in the second administration of Donald Trump. Perhaps we shouldn't care that a hedge fund billionaire like Bill Ackman believes a certain academic has engaged in plagiarism—except that he can expend millions of dollars amplifying his accusations against individuals and institutions, with potentially devastating consequences for the entire field of higher education. We might not care that Timothy Mellon harbors libertarian, anti-tax views, if he didn't also fund politicians and armies of lobbyists to alter U.S. tax laws to suit his financial interests—and in the process, deplete the public treasury available to the rest of society.

Still, the focus here is not on wealthy *individuals*; there are both scoundrels and generous souls among the lot. Instead, this book argues that an economy that is growing billionaires at all, much less at their current rate of increase, is *not* a sign of prosperity but of policy failure, resulting in a systemic problem with hugely consequential and negative impacts for society.

One sometimes hears sloppy chatter among pundits about "abolishing billionaires." That phrase has an exterminist whiff to it, which I believe should never be applied to people. Instead, I argue that we should focus on *abolishing a system of economic laws, rules, and practices* that funnels wealth to the top and undermines life for everyone else. And this is in large part because of the impact billionaires have on the rest of us. My invitation to you, as you read this book, is to consider the harms to you personally, perpetrated by an economic system that consolidates wealth and political power in a very few hands.

Of course, this is not solely a "billionaire problem." I argue that the greatest disruptions are driven by households in the top one-tenth of 1 percent—that is, those with more than $40 million in assets. This is the cohort that wealth managers call "ultra-high net worth" individuals. It is roughly at this point that wealth translates into levels of influence and power that distort democracy. Someone with $40 million has enough wealth to ensure that they and their heirs will lead lives of extreme comfort, security, and the ability to consume to suit their wildest desires. Above $40 million, wealth becomes sheer power: the influence to consolidate even more massive wealth, and the clout in policymaking spheres to protect and preserve it. This is the group this book refers to as "the billionaire class."

The billionaires overlap with and are sometimes indistinguishable from for-profit entities that are often the source of their wealth. Many billionaires have built their wealth through ownership and control of private equity firms and transnational corporations. Among the thirty largest private equity firms that assemble capital for the purchase of private companies (or the taking of public companies private), most are controlled by billionaires. Even when economic times are tough for the average American, the business leaders at the top tend to do not only fine but often better, by purchasing distressed companies or cornering the market on consumer access to needed goods.

Stephen Schwarzman, CEO of Blackstone Group, a private equity firm with over $1 trillion in assets, is personally worth $50.6 billion, up from a pre-pandemic wealth of $19.1 billion. George Roberts and Henry Kravis are billionaire cousins and co-directors of the private equity firm KKR, with $553 billion in client assets under management. Together, they control a fortune of $33.4 billion, up from a pre-pandemic $15.1 billion. Within the space of a year, between March 2020 and March 2021 (i.e., the nadir of COVID-19 job loss, illness, and death), the personal fortune of Amazon founder Jeff Bezos soared from $113 billion to $178 billion, a jump of 57 percent. All told, the total wealth of the world's billionaire class grew 54 percent during the first year of the pandemic.[3]

And billionaire power deeply affects you. Whether you are aware of it or not, where you live, what you eat, what news you consume, whether you feel economically secure, are all impacted by the billionaire class. Indeed, I argue that our current system of economic rules, laws, and practices is harming almost everyone by funneling huge amounts of society's bounty into the hands of a very few wealthy individuals.

Of course, I include stories and examples of billionaire excess to dramatize and underscore that individual behavior does sometimes matter. But it should not distract us from the more fundamental, dangerously systemic nature of the problem of wealth inequality—even if, in theory, a billionaire's wealth has been created through means that were not exploitative. Because wealth is power, excessive wealth in the hands of a few results in a harmful power imbalance; it gives a small group of people enormous weight to shape our society, culture, and economy, undermining democracy in the process.

The problem is not just that billionaires have excessive influence. With the assent of the U.S. Supreme Court's 2010 decision in *Citizens United v. Federal Election Commission*, which removed the guardrails around political contributions, billionaires are now achieving a virtual capture of our political system through their wealth, power, and position. Among

President-elect Trump's fifteen cabinet positions, eight of the nominees are billionaires.[4] Economists talk about the concept of "regulatory capture," when an oversight agency charged with protecting the public interest is dominated by the interests of the industry they are regulating.[5] Imagine the railroad owners regulating the railroads, to the detriment of passengers, customers, and people who live near the tracks: basically, the fox in charge of the proverbial henhouse. Billionaires have "captured" segments of our society and political system through money in politics, media ownership, and economic power.

In addition to political capture, I discuss the "wealth pump": the increasing siphoning of wages from the bottom 90 percent of income-earning households up to the top 1 percent—with the most gains of all flowing to the top 0.1 percent of multimillionaires and billionaires. Several historians have used the "wealth pump" metaphor to describe this hyper-extractive stage of capitalism, where more and more of society's wages and wealth are flowing into fewer hands.[6] The billionaire-backed private equity funds are an example of the wealth pump in action, as we will discuss throughout the book, in their ability to squeeze short-term wealth gains out of productive enterprises, often to the detriment and even bankruptcy of those companies.

According to a RAND Corporation analysis, if workers shared in productivity gains of their corporate employers (as they had between 1945 and 1974), they would have earned a combined additional average of $2.5 *trillion* a year.[7] Between 1975 and 2020, a total of $50 trillion in wages that should have been paid to the bottom 90 percent of households was funneled instead to the richest 1 percent—enough to pay every single working American in the bottom nine deciles an additional $1,144 a month. For every one of those forty-five years.

Imagine for a moment how the last few decades might have gone differently if workers had been paid those wages. As Nick Hanauer wrote in *Time* magazine, "That's $50 trillion that would have gone into the paychecks of working Americans had inequality held constant—$50 trillion that would have built a far larger and more prosperous economy—$50 trillion that would have enabled the vast majority of Americans to enter [the] pandemic far more healthy, resilient, and financially secure." Instead, we entered the COVID-19 pandemic in 2020 in a weakened state, with a vast number of Americans already living in economic precarity.[8]

This is just one concrete way in which the wealth pump and the extreme updraft of wealth undermine the security and well-being of the bottom 90 percent.

This book also makes an argument that might seem surprising: that extreme income inequality is bad for *everyone, including those in the billionaire class*. The excessively rich, too, live in an economically polarized society on an increasingly ecologically degraded Earth. Of course, because of their wealth, they will be shielded from the worst impacts of economic, social, and ecological disruption, at least in the short term. But it is not in the long-term interest of the billionaire classes to allow this system of extreme inequality of economic rewards to accelerate. Why? Because ultimately, oligarchies breed revolutions.

Historians such as Peter Turchin have pointed out that past societies that have produced great fortunes for the few and economic precarity for the many are not sustainable. Extreme wealth concentration not only is bad for ordinary working people and democracy in general but in extreme cases leads to social instability and breakdown. In his 2023 book, *End Times: Elites, Counter-Elites, and the Path of Political Disintegration,* Turchin chronicled the rise and fall of complex societies over the centuries. Societal collapse is often predicated on decades of wealth pumping upward into concentrations of wealth. This leads to what Turchin calls "elite overproduction," as a growing number of wealthy elite members and wannabes compete for a fixed and limited number of positions of power. In extreme cases, this leads to political polarization, disintegration, and a collapse of civil society. In the worst case, it fosters economic depression and war.[9]

HOW DOES BILLIONAIRE WEALTH INEQUALITY TOUCH YOU?

You may still be thinking, "So what? All that wealth accruing to the billionaires doesn't matter to me." But this book explores the very direct and personal ways that extreme concentrations of wealth and power touch your life: from trashing the environment and jeopardizing a livable future to increasing your tax bill, pushing up housing costs, putting your health at risk, robbing you of your political voice, and widening the racial economic divide. The drive by billionaires to amass ever greater wealth is warping the nonprofit sector, dictating what's on your dinner plate, and shaping the news you consume. It is even exploiting incarcerated people for profit—the ultimate captive market—and contributing to the further impoverishment of the most destitute people in our society.

We are being burned by billionaires.

* * * *

THIS BOOK IS DIVIDED into three sections. Part 1 explores the landscape of wealth and riches, the way great fortunes are accumulated, and the current picture of inequality. Part 2 provides an overview of how billionaire concentrations of wealth and power touch our lives in direct ways. Part 3 outlines the actions we can take to reverse our current course toward plutocratic power and rule. I'm a campaigner at heart, so I won't just report the bad news—I'll also describe the path forward to creating a healthier and more equal society.

We should all want a society that is not held hostage by the billionaire class: a society where everyone—not just the rich—can live with dignity, enjoy decent public services, and have the opportunity to thrive. People should be able to grow old in comfort, having lived a good and reasonably prosperous life. To achieve this vision of shared prosperity, it will be necessary to reduce inequality and achieve a society with fewer billionaires.

Part One

BILLIONAIRE WEALTH, POWER, AND INFLUENCE

CHAPTER 1

WHAT DO WE MEAN BY "THE WEALTHY"?

BEFORE INVESTIGATING THE HARMFUL IMPACT OF BILLIONaires on the rest of us, we need to start with an understanding of what we mean by "the wealthy." Are we talking about millionaires or billionaires? Income or assets? Is it the billionaire flying on a private jet to a Caribbean island? Or the neighbors up the street who always seem to have the flashiest new cars and posts of their latest exotic vacation on Facebook?

There is an obvious numerical distinction between a merely affluent household with a net worth of $1 million (including the equity in their home) and a billionaire, whose wealth can be measured in dollars and cents. But there is also a Grand Canyon of difference between these households in terms of political power, consumption, and influence, which is the subject of this book.

A key question in this conversation is, When does someone have *too much* wealth? At what point does someone have so much wealth that it exerts the power and influence to bend political institutions to his or her will in an undemocratic fashion—to lobby to rig the rules in their favor? What is mere "excess," and what is "excessive"? At what point are people done buying mansions and focused instead on buying senators?

The brief rebellion of the Occupy Wall Street movement in 2011, with its tagline about the richest 1 percent having more wealth than the bottom 99 percent, launched greater public scrutiny of wealth inequality. But as the introduction noted, most of the real growth in income and wealth since 2008 has flowed not to the richest 1 percent but to the *top one-tenth of 1 percent.*

"At some level of extreme wealth, money inevitably corrupts," observes columnist Farhad Manjoo. "On the left and the right, it buys political power, it silences dissent, it serves primarily to perpetuate ever-greater wealth, often unrelated to any reciprocal social good."[1]

If we fail to intervene in the system that is funneling wealth to the billionaires, we will create a hereditary aristocracy of wealth and power. On our current trajectory, a generation from now the children of today's billionaires will dominate our politics, economy, philanthropy, and culture. Imagine our lives in 2040 being almost entirely ruled by little Musks, Gateses, Buffetts, and Zuckerbergs.

You may be thinking, "Hasn't it always been this way? And aren't some of these billionaires generously giving away their money—even taking the Giving Pledge to donate half their wealth in their lifetime?" Indeed, historians can point to the first Gilded Age (roughly 1880–1915), in which vast fortunes were accumulated by the likes of the Rockefellers and Vanderbilts. But this Second Gilded Age has its own unique dynamics and distortions. We'll discuss charitable giving later in this book, as we look at the ways that philanthropy has become an extension of private billionaire wealth and influence—and moreover is not a substitute for a government tax system that affords members of the public meaningful input over allocations of public funds.

But wait. Aren't we ascribing too much power to a couple of thousand households? Other critics of inequality encourage us to widen our gaze to wealthy and affluent segments of society that lie between the wealthiest 0.1 percent and the top 9.9 percent below it. "The 9.9 Is the New American Aristocracy," Matthew Stewart writes in *The Atlantic*.[2] According to Stewart's widely read article (and later book), the big winners of the last several decades have indeed been the wealthiest 0.1 percent, with the big losers the bottom 90 percent of households. But the 9.9 percent group in between "has been doing just fine," holding ground in income and assets and using their cultural power to protect their advantages. The 9.9 percent, Stewart writes, "are mostly not like those flamboyant political manipulators from the 0.1 percent. We're a well-behaved, flannel-suited crowd of lawyers, doctors, dentists, mid-level investment bankers, MBAs with opaque job titles, and assorted other professionals—the kind of people who might invite you to dinner. . . . We keep insisting that we're 'middle class.'"[3]

Still others, like Brookings researcher Richard Reeves, argue that an even broader swath—the top 10 to 20 percent of the upper middle class—are "dream hoarders," using their privilege to hoard college access, erect "snob zoning" barriers to exclusive neighborhoods, and form professional associations that effectively function as cartels for high-paid occupations.[4] Others point to how "meritocratic" baby boomers have become "a protected class" by deploying the best and brightest of their generation to defend and multiply their assets and advantages.[5]

In a society slowly awakening to the complexities of class, this is a lot to absorb. Who is responsible for the greatest disruptions to our economic stability and quality of life? Where should we focus our attention to fix excessive inequality and its disruptions?

I argue in this book that the true drivers of inequality are the richest .01 percent of global citizens—in other words, the billionaires. This is not to ignore the role of a class of professional enablers and agents of these inequalities, many of whom reside in a stratum well below that of billionaires. As Stewart observes, the system wouldn't work without the cooperation of the affluent classes—"the staff that runs the machine that funnels resources from the 90 percent to the 0.1 percent." These folks have been happy to take their cut of the spoils.[6]

This upward funnel, or "wealth pump," is lubricated by a powerful narrative of meritocracy and "deservedness" that justifies these inequalities in the minds of the winners and often the losers as well. In a phrase, this is the belief that "people are where they deserve to be." Those with great wealth are deserving of it because of their hard work, intelligence, and entrepreneurial spirit. And those who are poor—well, they simply lack those virtues.

The über-wealthy wrap themselves in the ideology of meritocracy that is essential to legitimizing their wealth to themselves and society. And the merely affluent elite—who are mostly on the same team as the billionaire plutocrats—play a critical role in propagating this narrative of individual virtue and effort, not just to the masters of the universe at the top but to the bottom rungs of society as well.

THE GEOGRAPHY OF WEALTH

If the billionaires are driving the inequality express train, with lots of help from affluent segments of society, where are the pressure points for change? And what power and influence do the rest of the very wealthy wield?

One impediment to building effective social movements is that most of us don't entirely understand who the wealthy are. We still operate on caricatures and stereotypes that the wealthy look like Monopoly men, chubby little plutocrats wearing top hats and riding in chauffeur-driven limousines (instead of wearing hoodies and riding in self-driving Teslas). It is strategically important, however, to understand the different segments *within* the wealthy classes.

Journalist Robert Frank offered a helpful typology of the wealthy in his 2007 book, *Richistan: A Journey Through the American Wealth Boom and the Lives of the New Rich.*[7] To explain the distinctions, Frank divided the wealthy into several tiers of villages, what he called Lower Richistan, Middle Richistan, Upper Richistan—and Billionaireville.

I've modified and expanded Frank's concept, adding a few more neighborhoods. I've also updated his original statistics and added some of my own sociological markers. In my "road map," we look at income but mostly wealth and assets, because they tell us a lot more about status and power differentials.

There are varying data sets here—some apples, oranges, and few bananas thrown in—that make drawing an exact picture challenging. And there are, of course, serious limits to this type of topography. The experience of first-generation wealth holders is radically different from the experience of those who come from dynastic "old wealth." And there is a world of difference between a third-generation wealthy white family and a first-generation wealthy Black family. The source of one's wealth may create cultural differences in attitudes as divergent as those attendant to age, region, race, or religion. Disclaimers aside, here's a road atlas of Richistan.

Affluent Town

Affluent Town is home to those in the top 10 to 3 percent of American families. To live in Affluent Town, your annual household income must be roughly over $110,000, with wealth starting at $1.5 million. This group of more than 9 million households is a huge driving economic and cultural force in the United States, as these residents of Affluent Town own substantial property and financial assets.

While they are in every state, they are concentrated on the East and West Coasts and are clustered into about one hundred gilded zip codes. They occupy old wealth havens like Darien, Connecticut; Montclair, New Jersey; Scarsdale, New York; Weston, Massachusetts; and Winnetka, Illinois—and new wealth retirement towns like Jackson, Wyoming; and Pinecrest, Florida.[8]

Older residents of Affluent Town reside in the wealthy suburbs. But younger residents and retirees have become part of the new urban elite who have moved back into central cities, with a strong preference for high-tech knowledge hubs in coastal cities like San Francisco, Boston, Seattle, and New York City.[9]

Affluent Town is mostly white, but not entirely. Within the top 10 percent, 1.9 percent are Black and 2.4 percent are

Latino. Other racial groups including Asian individuals and multiracial individuals, account for 8.8 percent of Affluent Town.[10] With almost 10 million households that possess disposable income, they are huge engines of luxury consumption. They may sit in the coach section on commercial flights, but they probably own a BMW or Tesla that they replace every couple of years.

Members of Affluent Town are politically influential as compared to the bottom 90 percent. They are almost 100 percent registered to vote and are highly engaged in politics. They exercise their clout not just as voters but as campaign contributors. While the biggest donations to candidates rise as we climb higher up the mountain of Richistan, politically engaged residents of Affluent Town are among the 1.3 million donors that give between $200 and $2,699 in donations to candidates in major elections, for a total of $4 billion in the 2018 election cycle. While this group appears large, in truth only 0.48 percent of the population gives at this level.[11]

The clout of Affluent Town also comes through professional associations and bundled contributions through workplace PACs. Some members have personal relationships with local elected officials and maybe even national figures. They have probably lobbied their elected official on some matter.[12]

By most indicators, the residents of Affluent Town are "wealthy," though they may not feel that way. When they look up at the rest of Richistan, they see the threat of the economic precarity for themselves and their children were they to lose their job or a child fail to go to the right college. Overall, they are *very* concerned that their offspring don't lose economic status. As a result, they invest substantially in opening doors and expanding opportunities for their children. They invest in what sociologists call the "intergenerational transmission of advantage," a fancy way of saying they massage their networks to get their kids into the right schools, internships, and summer jobs in order to position them for success in today's economy.

The overall focus of life in Affluent Town is status preservation. Their gaze is upward, aspiring to more prosperous villages and working to protect their interests. In fact, many residents of Affluent Town are employed in occupations that serve the wealthier segments of society, particularly in legal or financial services, otherwise known as the "wealth defense industry." They staff the law, accounting, and wealth management firms, the "family offices," charitable foundations, impact investing funds, and other professional service organizations that largely serve the upper echelons of Richistan. For this reason, policies that pressure the wealthy to pay more taxes will be viscerally opposed in Affluent Town—not because they will directly pay those higher rates of taxes—but because they know where their bread is buttered.

Lower Richistan

Lower Richistan includes approximately 2.6 million households with wealth between $6 million and $13 million. This is the top 3 percent of wealth holders, excluding the wealthiest 1 percent.[13] The annual income of Lower Richistanis ranges from $180,000 to $300,000.[14]

The income and wealth of this group comes from business ownership, salaries, stock investments, and inheritances. This diverse group shares many affluent suburban zip codes and urban enclaves with inhabitants of Affluent Town.

Lower Richistanis are among the political influencers and donors, a group that grows as income and wealth rise. They are increasingly moving back into city centers, driving up the cost of urban real estate. These are the people who populate upscale restaurants, country clubs, and luxury vacation destinations. They likely have second homes. They still fly on commercial airlines but sometimes sit in first class.

This group also includes an older "boomer" generation of "millionaire-next-door" households, folks whose wealth grew steadily in the decades after World War II, thanks to small-business ownership and long-term investments. These next-door millionaires are the opposite of flashy ostentatious wealth, often living in their first homes and leading relatively thrifty lives.[15]

Lower Richistanis are more economically cushioned and secure than residents of Affluent Town. They are less anxious about the downward mobility of their children yet are not as deeply disconnected from the rest of society as residents of Upper Richistan.

Middle Richistan

Middle Richistan is inhabited by almost 1.3 million households that represent the top 1 percent of wealth holders—excluding the .01 percent of billionaires. The wealthiest 1 percent have assets over $13 million, with an average $37 million in wealth.

The wealth of Middle Richistanis derives from business ownership, investments, and some earned income. These are people who have benefited hugely from four decades of tax cuts and other public policies that have enriched asset owners at the expense of wage earners. There is an enormous range in property and assets between the top and bottom of Middle Richistan, meaning that some have just one country home while others have several. At the upper end of Middle Richistan, residents fly on private jets or own fractional interests in private planes through businesses like NetJets.

Upper Richistan

Upper Richistan is home to roughly 130,000 American households with wealth ranging from $60 million to $1 billion. Their annual incomes start at about $1 million and go up. This group received more than 90 percent of the gains in income and wealth produced since the Great Recession of 2008.[16]

Households in Upper Richistan have enough money to cover life's luxuries and ensure themselves against most adversity. They can set their children up with trust funds at birth and raise them in bubbles of privilege. Upper Richistanis own multiple properties in urban, suburban, and luxury vacation destinations, ensuring that they are ensconced in a bubble of luxury wherever they travel around the globe. This class of wealthy people have multiple homes but invest in additional luxury real estate in order to diversify their holdings, rather than as residences (discussed in chapter 6). Accumulating further wealth in Upper Richistan is mainly an exercise in building power and compounding an already luxurious standard of creature comforts.

As a class, Upper Richistanis and billionaires are huge political influencers, donating substantially to all the campaign outlets available to them. Some of these political contributions are reported, but under the surface are large icebergs of dark money influence: huge amounts of cash that flow through hidden financial vehicles, including the increasing use of non-profit advocacy organizations that are not required to disclose their donors.[17]

Parenting is a challenge for all people in every class stratum, and this is true in Richistan. Wealth does not buffer families from divorce, disability, addiction, and other adversities. But there are so many other resources to be deployed to support Richistani children that they are more likely to overcome them. These include tutors, personal coaches, treatment clinics, pharmacological aids, college counselors, therapeutic boarding schools, pricey summer camps, and all manner of high-priced enrichment programs.

The pursuit of admission to selective colleges is important to Upper Richistanis. Unlike those in Affluent Town, this is sought less as a hedge against downward mobility and more as a means of maintaining and enhancing family status. Nonetheless, all Richistanis deploy significant resources in tilting the college admission process in their children's favor. For Lower Richistanis, this could mean living in an affluent community with high property taxes and significant investments in public schools that are mostly reserved for the children of the wealthy. But even in communities with excellent public schools, the Upper Richistanis are sending their kids to private schools.

Private schools are, as the writer Matthew Stewart observes, the "mother lode of all affirmative action programs for the wealthy." Only 2.2 percent of the nation's students graduate from nonreligious private high schools, yet they account for 26 percent of students enrolled at Harvard and 28 percent of students at Princeton.[18] At some of these private high schools, annual tuition costs as much as a year of college. As Stewart writes, “Throw in the counselors, the whisperers, the violin lessons, the private schools, and the cost of arranging for Junior to save a village in Micronesia, and it adds up.”

At the top of Upper Richistan are the folks approaching billionaire status. Their ranks include heirs to multigenerational wealth dynasties, alongside first-generation entrepreneurs, hedge fund managers, and CEOs (though many CEOs still work for a living, something some of the heirs have not experienced). Together with the billionaires, they make election-shifting donations to political candidates and super PACs. They are no doubt overrepresented among the ranks of dark money donors, whose activities we are unable to track.

This group thinks generationally about wealth and assets. As Frank writes, “When you live in Upper Richistan, your entire philosophy of money changes. You realize that you can’t possibly spend all your fortune, or even part of it, in your lifetime and that your money will probably grow over the years even if you spend lavishly. So Upper Richistanis plan their finances for the next hundred years. They don’t buy mutual funds; they buy timber land, oil rigs and office towers.”[19]

Those in Upper Richistan and Billionaireville live in a parallel universe of privilege, disconnected from the plight and concerns of ordinary working people, unless they choose to connect as a matter of charity. Some have philanthropic foundations that serve as proxies for their concerns, and which occasionally put them in contact with the planet’s most needy. Some are eloquent allies for reducing poverty, though rarely do they advocate for fairer taxation.

Billionaireville

Finally, at the very top of the mountain of Richistan lies Billionaireville—the tiny and exclusive enclave of roughly eight hundred American billionaires, all of whom also reside on the *Forbes* list of richest people in the world.[20] According to best estimates, American billionaires own a combined wealth of more than $7 trillion, or *more than half the wealth of the entire rest of the United States' 65 million households, combined.*[21] (Because many conceal their wealth in complex trusts and offshore bank accounts, an accurate estimation of their true wealth is impossible to ascertain.)

Like their neighbors just down the hill in Upper Richistan, the billionaires take a long view of most financial and life

I LOVE THE FOUR SEASONS,.. MANHATTAN, PALM BEACH, PARIS AND MARTHA'S VINEYARD.

endeavors. They own multiple properties and move on a seasonal basis from one luxury compound to the next, with personnel flying ahead to prepare dinner. From New York City and Los Angeles to Sundance and Sun Valley, from Palm Springs to Palm Beach, the migrations of the very wealthy are tied to social events, sunshine, peak powder, and high culture.

The income of Billionaireville comes almost entirely from capital income—earnings from ownership of assets and capital gains—not in the form of a weekly paycheck. Unlike the tuxedo-clad elites of generations past, many denizens of Billionaireville pad about their homes and offices in an unassuming uniform of T-shirts and jeans.

Some are still actively making money, especially those in new media, technology, and finance. These are the founders of hedge funds and technology companies like Google, Amazon, and Facebook. Others are members of American wealth dynasties like the Walton, Koch, and Mars (candy) families. The concentration of wealth in Billionaireville is growing such that it is likely to produce its first trillionaire by 2030.[22]

At this level of wealth, families focus on multigenerational legacies, landholdings, and philanthropic institutions. Left unhindered, the children of today's billionaires will become a hereditary aristocracy of wealth and power.

Dynastic Wealth Among the Billionaires

While some residents of Billionaireville are owners of large private companies, most of their orientation is toward dynastic wealth preservation. In healthy societies with functioning tax systems, wealth disperses over generations, tracking the maxim of "from shirtsleeves to shirtsleeves in three generations." The first generation builds wealth, the second generation pays taxes and spends the money such that by the third generation, people are back to working for a living. Dynasty-building billionaire families have arrested this process of wealth diffusion. Instead, their wealth is growing over generations, piling up more treasure than they can possibly use in their lifetimes.

* * * *

THIS GEOGRAPHY OF WEALTH hopefully illustrates the varying gradations and priorities of the people we consider "wealthy." While there is tremendous influence and clout among the top 10 percent of affluent and wealthy households, the most significant degree of political, economic, and cultural power resides among the top 0.1 percent. The greatest harms to our lives are largely driven by the residents of Upper Richistan and Billionaireville: those occupying the very richest echelons of wealth.

CHAPTER 2

HOW DO PEOPLE BECOME BILLIONAIRES?

THE ACCUMULATION OF WEALTH IN THE HANDS of the few has accelerated markedly over the past four decades. Yet most of the public has no concept of just how excessively wealthy the rich are. First, some level-setting math: a billion is one thousand million dollars. Between 1980 and 2024, the number of billionaires in the United States has increased fifty times, from fifteen to more than eight hundred.

How did this massive accumulation of wealth happen? In overview, the four primary stages of wealth accumulation are as follows:

* Wealth accumulation (assembling a fortune)
* Wealth defense (defending a fortune and fending off competition)
* Political capture (rigging the rules to get more)
* Hyper-extraction (siphoning more wealth by preying on the economic precarity of the bottom 90 percent)

Cycle of billionaire wealth concentration

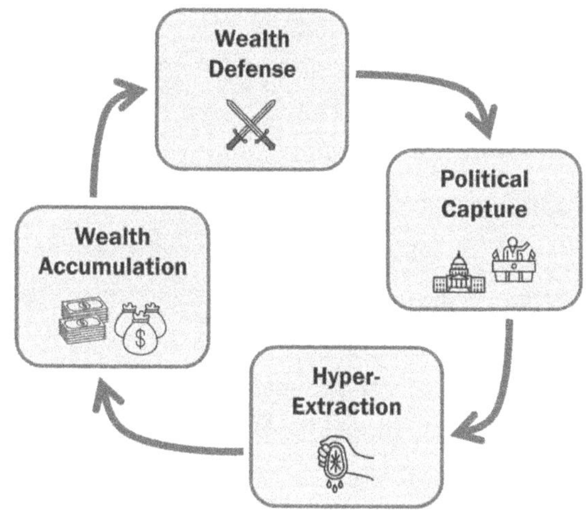

Adapted from the Excessive Wealth Disorder Institute

STAGE ONE: WEALTH ACCUMULATION

How do I make my first billion and move to Billionaireville? Wouldn't you like to know! There are a variety of theories about how someone can accumulate a lot of wealth—and of course, many books, courses, and rags-to-riches biographies on offer that purport to show you how.[1]

People have various euphemisms for this stage, including "wealth creation," "accumulation," and "wealth extraction." Each has embedded political assumptions and narratives. "Wealth creation" suggests a narrative of *virtuous wealth* in which an individual brings qualities of grit, sacrifice, intelligence, and hard work to a successful enterprise. They invent "a better mousetrap," and people are willing to part with their money to have it. This is the altar of meritocracy to which we are typically urged to bow.

"Wealth extraction," by contrast, implies a "cornering of the market" or exploitative arrangement. Early fortunes were formed by settlers who initially became wealthy by seizing or accumulating land, the original form of wealth. Often, they could work this land profitably because they had free or low-cost labor in the form of enslaved people, indentured servants, or impoverished immigrant workers. Honoré de Balzac once said, "Behind every great fortune lies a great crime."[2] And indeed, historically, there are many examples of great fortunes accumulated through criminal and/or immoral activities, or violently enforced monopolies.

While many people became prosperous and wealthy by digging, harvesting, and hunting, the great fortunes came about by dominating the market through monopoly control of the product or key infrastructure. These monopolies, or what were called "combinations" and "trusts" at the turn of the twentieth century, were connected to Gilded Age families and generally pertained to extraction of minerals or other natural resources like copper, gold, silver, oil, timber, plant dyes, animal skins, cod, and beef, or were achieved by controlling major transportation infrastructure, like railroads and shipping.

In this phase, it's easier to comprehend the "extractive" nature of the enterprises. What could be more "extractive" than mining, slaughtering beavers, and cutting down trees? And within these early industries, one can readily grasp the "extraction of labor value," as the Marxists call it, in the exploitation of workers. Whole industries like cotton were built on enslaved or sharecropper labor. Miners, lumberjacks, and

Match the dynastic family to its source of wealth:

Match the billionaire to their source of wealth:

industrial workers fought back against exploitive conditions and lost life and limb fighting for dignified working conditions and livable wages. Farmers have historically been squeezed by monopoly seed companies, equipment vendors, transport barons, and commodity price markets. And some farming depends on an extractive agriculture model of taking more from the soil than is replaced in the form of nutrients.

In this, our Second Gilded Age (running roughly from the 1980s to the present), most new billionaire fortunes have been accrued through the invention of new technologies connected to the internet and computers. Starting in the 1990s, huge fortunes emerged through the development of computer hardware and software (Intel, Microsoft, Apple), internet-based social media companies (Facebook, YouTube, Instagram), online shopping (Amazon), and tech-based personal services like Uber, Lyft, and Airbnb.

In our modern tech economy, one becomes wealthy by inventing a useful technology and then setting up a "tollbooth" to collect a transaction fee every time someone uses one's technology. Some economists analogize this to charging "rent" in the form of a fee from those who wish to access a service on a "platform" of digital real estate, for example, for the purposes of ordering food on the Grubhub app. And when there is a crisis that drives up demand—such as the COVID-19 pandemic—these rent seekers are well positioned to extract even greater profits from ordinary workers or consumers. Think Zoom.

Billionaire fortunes surged during the first part of the pandemic as consumers shut inside their homes conducted work meetings online, bought groceries, ordered takeout, and built that back deck they'd always wanted through online retailers. Between mid-March 2020 and October 2021, the combined wealth of our nation's then 745 billionaires jumped from $3 trillion to $5.1 trillion, a gain of $2.1 trillion, or more than 70 percent. A year later, in October 2022, total billionaire wealth had declined somewhat, to $4.48 trillion, but this was still a 50 percent gain over where things stood before the beginning of the pandemic.[3] The biggest gains were among owners of cloud-based technologies, online retailers, and delivery applications.

DoorDash is one of several cloud-based apps that matches hungry people to the real economy of restaurants and delivery people. The companies that operate food delivery apps are quintessential middlemen: they don't do any of the real work of growing the food, preparing it, or driving about at all hours of the day and night delivering it. They don't even pay for the delivery vehicle or its gas. But they do collect a fee for every transaction that matches a customer to a restaurant and driver. And in some markets, they effectively drive down profits for food producers and wages for delivery people, by creating a larger competition bidding space in which restaurants and workers compete to win more customers by charging less.[4]

When people were sequestered in their homes during the COVID-19 pandemic, without the ability to either go outside or enjoy a meal in a restaurant, the market for these online food delivery apps skyrocketed, creating instant billionaires of their owners.[5] The three founders of DoorDash each saw their wealth hit $2.5 billion (later, after the pandemic eased and competition increased, their stock market wealth dropped back to earthly levels). Matt Maloney, who founded Grubhub, sold the food software app to a European conglomerate, Just Eat, for $7.3 billion. Many people will argue that these apps and enterprises are useful and convenient. But these billion-dollar enterprises are also extractive: they feed off the slim margins of restaurants, which pay a portion of their profits to apps like Grubhub and Uber Eats to compete for takeout business. Meanwhile, the delivery drivers for these gig corporations compete with one another for low wages, essentially depending on tips to survive.[6]

In both the old and the new Gilded Ages of extreme inequality, we find the so-called FIRE sector—finance, insurance, and real estate—thriving by skimming fortunes from the productive economy. During the past forty years of accelerating inequality, the financial sector has expanded at a greater rate than other segments of the economy (like manufacturing or services), in what some economists describe as "financialization." This sector has become parasitical, extracting wealth from the economy of regular goods and services to funnel wealth up to investors and owners. As Americans, we love to complain about taxes, but we don't always contemplate the private form of taxes we pay to corporations in the form of junk fees attached to bills for cable, internet, insurance, banking, mobile phone, and ticket purchases. At every step through your day, whether online or on Main Street, some billionaire is picking your pocket.

People create modest wealth through starting businesses, landing them in Affluent Town, but the real fortunes of Upper Richistan are formed when these enterprises reach market brand dominance with large production and distribution networks. If you have any doubt about this, just look at the share of the market controlled by five large food and beverage conglomerates, PepsiCo, Tyson, Nestlé, JBS, and Kraft Heinz.[7]

In short, the initial accumulation phase is the stage where an individual moves from relatively modest means to owning and controlling substantial wealth by engaging in some successful enterprise where wealth flows to them. In the most classic and benign form, they have created or invented something that lots of people are willing to pay for.

In my town, there is a guy named Tito who makes an amazing burrito. He used to sell them out of a cooler on a street corner, then he set up a cart at the edge of a supermarket parking lot. A year later, he had a food truck. People lined up for Tito's burritos. He was so successful that he leased an old gas station and opened a restaurant with an expanded menu. Today, he has several franchise locations and Tito's Tacos are a favorite local business. Tito has not (yet) become a billionaire, but he's come a long way from selling burritos out of a cooler. And he has achieved a level of economic security and stability that has landed him in Affluent Town. He has employees, payroll costs, and probably most of the headaches associated with operating a small or medium-size business.[8]

His is a story of meritocratic rise. But Tito is not likely to become a billionaire, even if he sells his three-restaurant franchise to Chipotle. He won't be able to command monopoly power. Nonetheless, this is the classic story of wealth "creation" that gets projected onto the popular narrative of meritocracy. Many billionaires love to tell their humble origin stories (if they have one) because such accounts reinforce the notion that their wealth is "deserved"—that is, rooted solely in their individual achievement.

STAGE TWO: WEALTH DEFENSE

Regardless of the story we favor about the initial accumulation phase of wealth, at a certain point, those with rapidly accumulating wealth turn their attention to strategies to preserve and defend their assets, and to minimize competition for their profit-making enterprises. Sometimes this process doesn't fully engage until the second or third generation in a family. First-generation entrepreneurs are often less focused on wealth defense because they are still leading enterprises involved in accumulating wealth. But subsequent generations are not as confident in their wealth-creation capacities and focus tremendous energy and resources on holding on to what they have, including by hiring professional help.

Whenever wealth holders shift from accumulation to defense, they engage the services of what we call the "wealth defense industry." These are the tax lawyers, accountants, and wealth managers who deploy their considerable expertise to help sequester the wealth of their clients outside the reach of tax authorities, ex-spouses, hapless heirs, litigious people, and other perceived threats.

In 2021, I published a book called *The Wealth Hoarders: How Billionaires Pay Millions to Hide Trillions.* (It probably would have sold better if I'd titled it *How to Hide Your First Billion.*) For the book, I interviewed dozens of professionals in the wealth defense industry, some of them itching to "tell all" and defect. Since the publication of the book, more have approached me to validate my analysis and share more examples. What I describe here is based on their insights.

As mentioned in the earlier discussion of Billionaireville, families with substantial wealth (usually over $150 million) may form a so-called family office to bring wealth management services in-house, retaining privacy and control over substantial assets. Family offices are a growing unregulated space, as they successfully fended off oversight after the 2009 economic meltdown and the Dodd-Frank financial reform act. As a result, some wealthy hedge fund operators are converting their businesses to family offices to escape even the minimal scrutiny to which they are now subject.[9]

The wealth defense industry—including family office staffers—typically measure their success by three benchmarks:

* **Growth** of assets—encouraging the growth of the corpus of wealth through savvy investments

* **Tax minimization**—using myriad strategies to avoid or reduce taxes

* **Dynastic succession**—maximizing the amount of wealth flowing to blood heirs

To accomplish these objectives, wealth defense professionals use a wide variety of tools, such as trusts, offshore bank accounts, anonymous shell companies, charitable foundations, and other vehicles, to hold assets. They will also use a variety of complex transactions, tax loopholes, and financial shell games to further advance their clients' interests. Regulatory complexity is their strong suit, as they shift wealth to a series of shadowy, opaque ownership vehicles and to jurisdictions with the least amount of accountability, reporting, and taxation.

The wealth defense industry will tell you that they are just "helping families." In fact, they are helping a tiny sliver of the wealthiest families on the planet, at the expense of every other family. They will also claim they are "aiding their clients to obey and comply with existing laws." But this masks how segments of this industry are actively writing the laws, by lobbying for changes in state and federal rules and regulations to advance their clients' interests.[10] In addition to advocating for tax cuts, they are creating complicated new trust configurations and ownership entities to hide wealth.[11]

The trust industry has effectively captured state trust law in a dozen states in the United States, including Texas, Florida, and Delaware, allowing for the creation of dynasty trusts and anonymous shell companies with no or low tax obligations. These are known as "trust haven states."[12] The trust industry also holds enormous sway in tax haven territories like the Cayman Islands, Bermuda, and the British Virgin Islands, where a large part of their jurisdictional business revolves around hiding the wealth of the billionaire class. These jurisdictions are engaged in a race to the bottom, competing with one another to place the fewest requirements and taxes on wealth depositors, trust holders, and company owners.

The wealth defense industry has also literally reworked trust law to create new mutations of trusts to encourage wealth to flow down the narrow generational line. Several states, such as South Dakota, Wyoming, and Nevada, are now desirable jurisdictions for "dynasty trusts," where assets can be held for generations—tax-free and anonymously—in order to avoid the estate tax, which has long been a thorn in the side of the very wealthy.[13] For the residents of Billionaireville, the estate tax is now a joke, a porous and largely irrelevant tax. This is a concrete measure of success for the wealth defense industry, which has weakened the estate tax as a brake on intergenerational wealth transfers that once prevented (or at least slowed) the consolidation of wealth dynasties.

STAGE THREE: POLITICAL CAPTURE

Wealth over $40 million translates into substantial power. This third stage involves the consolidation of plutocratic power over democratic and economic institutions, what I described in the introduction as "political capture." In other words, the billionaire class "captures" the law-writing and law enforcement roles of our democracy by exerting tremendous influence over legislators and government executives as political donors, media owners, and powerhouses with sway over the economy. This enables the excessively wealthy to rig the rules of the economy in favor of wealth defense and additional accumulation.

At this stage of wealth, many billionaires are highly engaged in politics, elections, and policy matters, actively influencing the rules and narratives of the economy. Some oligarchs are aggressively pursuing a wealth protection and expansion agenda, deploying every tool in their influence toolbox. These include political donations to electoral candidates and PACs; donations to dark money nonprofit advocacy organizations; tax-exempt donations to qualified charities engaged in research and advocacy to advance the donor's interests; for-profit investments in media ownership; and many more.

Powerful donors like the Koch family on the right and George Soros on the left have figured out how to align and weaponize every aspect of their wealth to advance their interests. In many cases, this includes blocking legislative and policy changes that may be widely popular, thus imposing a form of "minority rule" by the wealthy. For example, the Kochs have funded successful campaigns to block popular antipollution legislation from passing, while the Soros family has funded projects focused on drug decriminalization and criminal justice reform that have outpaced public opinion.[14]

My colleague at the Institute for Policy Studies Sam Pizzigati has written for decades about the capture of our political system by the excessively wealthy. "In a democracy, people identify the problems they face and, working together, try to fashion solutions," writes Sam. "In a plutocracy, by contrast, a society's richest employ their power to exploit the most pressing problems their nation faces—and keep real solutions off the table."[15]

What sometimes plays out in our political sphere is often a clash of liberal versus libertarian versus conservative billionaire titans with opposing agendas. This is what historian Peter Turchin describes as an example of "intra-elite conflict" and competition between subsets of the wealth and power elite contesting a shrinking number of positions of power and influence.[16]

STAGE FOUR: HYPER-EXTRACTION

The fourth stage in this cycle could be described as the "hyper-extraction" phase, as billionaires prey upon the rest of society, including those disadvantaged by decades of inequality.

One recent example is the trillions of dollars of investment capital moving into the purchase of single-family rental homes or real estate investment trusts for short-term rentals, which removes affordable rental housing from the market. In this way, wealth inequality has worsened a substantial housing crisis, pushing the cost of affordable housing out of reach. But in stage four, hyper-extraction, wealthy investors extract additional value from those backed up in rental housing. Families that in the previous generation would have been able to purchase a home are stuck in the rental market. For billionaire investors in real estate, this creates another "rent-seeking" opportunity for profit.

We also see this kind of predatory activity in the form of private equity billionaires buying up hospitals and even telecommunications for prisoners.

A segment of the very wealthy may be content with a "capital preservation" strategy, directing their wealth defense industry minions to diversify holdings outside of public stock markets and into geographically distributed land and housing, artwork, jewelry, cryptocurrency, and other assets. This sort of billionaire family may be content that their fortune holds its value, grows modestly, and generates income down the generational line.

But where there is great wealth, there are usually multiple investment strategies, including allocating a portion of the wealth management operation to focus on aggressive growth and financial returns. For these folks, annual asset growth or an investment return of less than 10 percent is considered a defeat, a source of shame almost equivalent to a tax bill approaching the national tax rate of 13.63 percent.[17] (The effective tax rate on individuals on the Forbes 400 list of the largest billionaires was 8.2 percent between 2010 and 2018, much lower than the tax rate for a teacher or nurse.)[18]

To achieve high financial returns or significant asset growth requires walking through the door marked "Casino." Not literally a Las Vegas casino, but the part of capital markets that is highly speculative and risky, with the potential for substantial returns. Even if only 15 or 20 percent of a billionaire's investments are in high-risk speculative vehicles, that's $150 million or $200 million chasing high returns.

These supercharged investment returns are often obtained through hyper-extractive investments in real estate, hedge funds, and private equity that take advantage of scarcities and vulnerabilities in the market. For example, the amount of private equity wealth moving into the speculative edge of the market is substantial. As you'll see from several of the examples that follow, billionaire-backed private equity is actively extracting wealth from housing, health care, veterinary care, prisons, and any other corner of the economy where there is money to be made. The private equity playbook usually involves cutting costs, severing assets such as real estate from the business service, squeezing wages from workers, depressing prices from suppliers, and raising costs on customers, while grabbing huge fees in the process. Economist Eileen Appelbaum, author of several studies and a book on private equity, observes that while there are four thousand private equity funds in the United States, the largest thirty of them are the heavyweights, managing several trillion dollars in investment assets. They load up a company with debt, writes Appelbaum, "and then they have to be able to both pay back that debt and get outsized returns—20 percent is what they go for—for their investors."[19] Oxford professor Ludovic Phalippou described private equity as a "factory for billionaires."[20]

* * * *

THE PROCESS OF ACCUMULATING wealth described in the previous section is what historian Peter Turchin calls the "wealth pump," by which wealth is siphoned from low- and middle-income households up to the wealthiest 1 percent and higher. In medieval societies, he explains, there was coercion involved in pumping wealth upward: think feudal landholding arrangements, war, and old-fashioned plunder. In modern societies, this manifests as stagnating wages, which are the result of elites "reconfiguring the economy in their interests."[21]

History teaches that there are almost always political costs to be paid from excessive extractions of wealth. Turchin documents that extreme imbalances of power and wealth eventually generate social unrest, political disintegration, and "the rise of counter-elites." Or as William Bernstein, the author of a recent article titled "The Wealth Pump," observes, "stable, wealthy societies invariably accrue, like barnacles on a ship, layers of rent-seeking elites who tear apart societies by creaming off a nation's riches."[22]

Each of the four stages of the wealth accretion process contributes to different harms. In the initial accumulation phase, the run-up in wealth may be the result of uncompetitive, monopolistic businesses, which can extract higher fees for their service. In the wealth defense phase, professional enablers manipulate laws and the investment environment to sequester wealth outside taxation and accountability. In essence, they are the contractors building the ramparts and moats around Upper Richistan and Billionaireville.

In the political capture phase, extreme wealth translates into the exercise of power, usually to advance the wealth accumulation agenda of the billionaire class. The final phase, hyper-extraction, sees the billionaire class take advantage of wealth disparities and power imbalances to extract additional wealth gains at the expense of the rest of society.

Within the United States, we lack a ready vocabulary to describe what this concentration of wealth and power does to our society. Words like "oligarchy" (rule by the few) or "plutocracy" (rule by the wealthy) are accurate but entirely inadequate descriptors of the overall repressive and depressive impact of extreme inequality. In truth, societies dominated by hereditary wealth and power harken back to feudalism.

CHAPTER 3

WHAT CREATED SO MANY BILLIONAIRES?

SINCE 1983, THE CLUB OF U.S. BILLIONAIRES HAS INCREASED from fifteen individuals to more than eight hundred.[1] How exactly did this happen? Before we dive in to answer that question, let's first start with a friendly quiz that may prove surprising.

1. In 1980, the ratio between CEO pay among the Fortune 500 and average worker pay was 42 to 1. In 2023, the ratio between CEOs and average workers at the five hundred biggest public companies was:[2]

A. 55 to 1
B. 412 to 1
C. More than 1,000 to 1
D. 268 to 1
E. 125 to 1

2. The U.S. estate tax is the only federal levy on inherited wealth. In 2025, the tax exempts people with what level of wealth?[3]

A. Under $500,000 ($1 million per couple)
B. Under $7 million ($14 million per couple)

C. Under $14 million ($28 million per couple)
D. Under $50 million ($100 million per couple)

3. The richest 10 percent of U.S. households owned what percentage of all stock market wealth in 2023?[4]

A. 35 percent
B. 46 percent
C. 71 percent
D. 93 percent

4. What percentage of all U.S. households have zero financial reserves (i.e., zero or negative net worth)?[5]

A. 10
B. 15
C. 20
D. 30

5. What percentage of Black households have zero or negative net worth?[6]

A. 15
B. 20
C. 25
D. 30

[Answers: 1: D; 2: C; 3: D; 4: B; 5: C]

Congratulations if you got even half of these answers right; most people don't. Public opinion research indicates that most Americans greatly underestimate the levels of inequality that exist in the United States.[7] Most of us don't fly on private jets or get invited to Richard Branson's island paradise, so we have only a fleeting sense of just how rich the excessively wealthy have become.

The reality is that in a relatively short span of time, the United States has become a deeply unequal society, with an increasingly greater share of the nation's treasure consolidated into a small number of hands. How did this billionaire boom come to pass, exactly?

There are essentially three economic forces driving the billionaire expansion: the suppression of wages for average working people (even as those workers became more productive); the meteoric rise in the stock market; and massive tax cuts for the wealthiest households that accelerated in the Reagan area and have continued to the present day.[8]

If you're under the age of fifty, you've lived your entire adult life during a period of growing, extreme inequality. When you tell today's college graduates about the U.S. government's investments in debt-free college and low-interest loans for first-time homebuyers between 1945 and 1979, you might as well be talking about life on a utopian planet (or maybe in a Scandinavian nation).

Following are a few specially chosen data points and graphs that help illustrate the unequal times we are living through.

INCOME

Productivity Versus Wage Growth

If I was going to show you only one chart to exemplify the dynamics of the wealth pump, the chart that follows would be it. What you see here is the gradual delinking of wages from productivity. In this graph, you can see that worker productivity rose steadily in the decades after World War II—1948 to 1979. During this period, worker productivity increased 117.5 percent, more than doubling over three decades. Compensation of workers rose in tandem, increasing 107.3 percent. In other words, workers during this period shared in the productivity gains to which they contributed.

Then around 1979, we begin to see a growing divergence between productivity and pay, with productivity continuing to rise 64.7 percent while wages flatlined, growing only 14.8 percent over the period 1979 to 2022.[9] Where did the profits from this

Worker Productivity and Wages Become Delinked

Productivity/growth and hourly compensation growth by quarter, 1948–2023, indexed to 1948 values

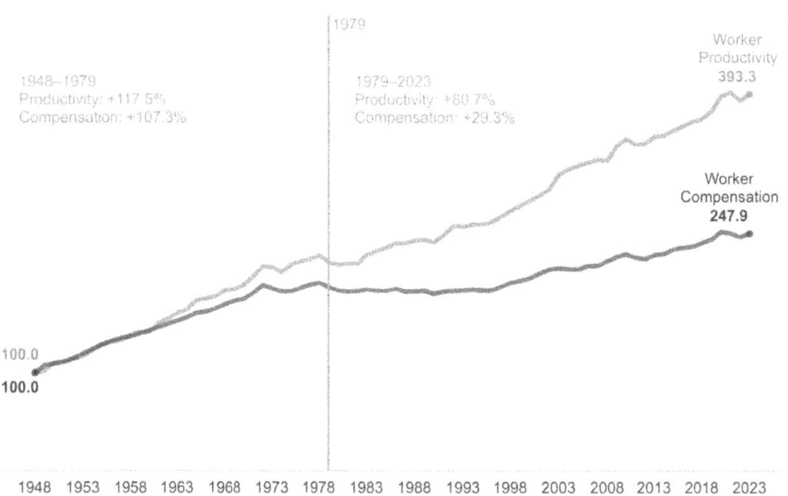

Source: "The Productivity Pay Gap" by the Economic Policy Institute.

increased productivity go? Well, in sum, productivity gains since 1979 have flowed to shareholder investors—that is, to owners of assets like stock—and not to wage earners. This is the essence of the modern wealth pump in action.

As a result of the "shared prosperity" economy in the decades after World War II, the distribution of wage growth was quite equitable across each quintile, or fifth, of the economy. The bottom fifth of households, the middle, and the top fifth all moved in tandem.

In the decades after 1979, we see a pulling apart of these groups, with income gains flowing to the top fifth and top 1 percent.

Another important part of the story is to look at this recent period of inequality and compare it to 120 years ago, during

In the Decades After World War II, Incomes Grew Together. Since 1979, We Have Pulled Apart

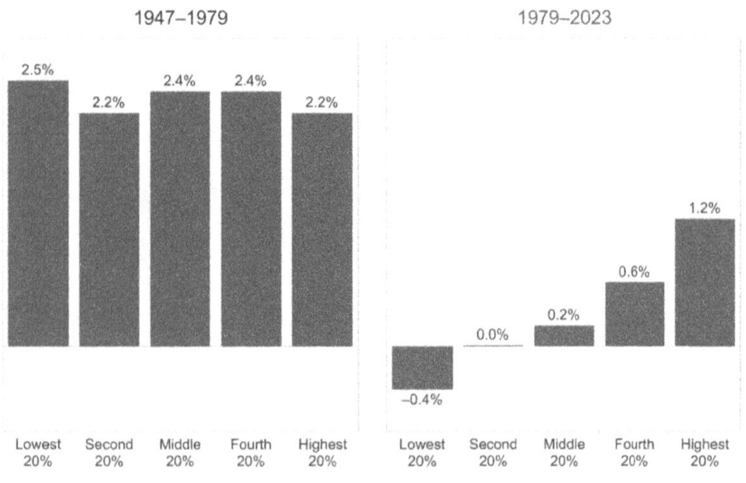

Source: Data from the Current Population Survey of the U.S. Census Bureau.

Income Concentration Over the Last Century

Share of total U.S. income going to households in the top 0.1% and top 0.01% income levels, 1918–2018

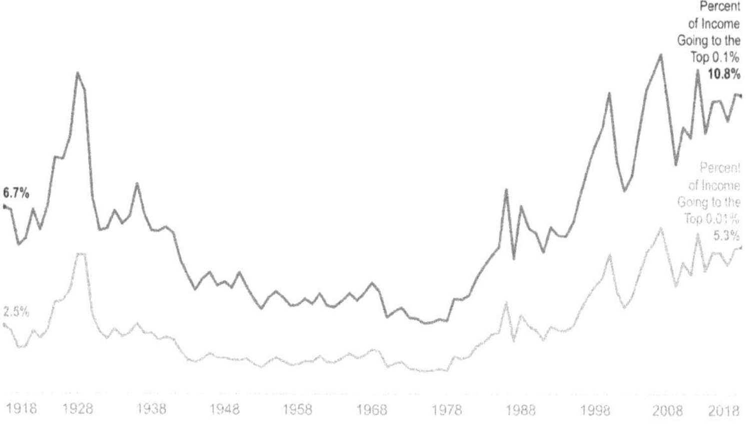

Source: "Striking It Richer: The Evolution of Top Incomes in the United States" by Emmanuel Saez, University of California at Berkeley, February 2020.

the first Gilded Age—the last time income gains were steeply updrafted to the top of the wealth pyramid. As the previous chart shows, the gains to the top .01 percent are the driving force pushing up the share flowing to the top 1 percent.

STOCK MARKET WEALTH

Wealth, rather than income, tells an even deeper and multigenerational story of inequality, including the legacy of racial discrimination in wealth building. The next chart illustrates the growth in the number of billionaires since 2003 and their increases in wealth during the 2020 to 2022 pandemic.

For most U.S. households, if they own any wealth, it is in the form of modest retirement savings and maybe some equity in a home. The focus on the stock market is overhyped as an indicator of economic health because it is not so relevant to many households, even those that have retirement savings in mutual fund portfolios managed by their employers. Nor is it important from the perspective of job creation.[10]

But the U.S. stock market *is* where major wealth gains have occurred and is largely a sandbox of the already rich. According to Siblis Research, the estimated valuation of all publicly traded companies in the U.S. stock market in July 2024 was $55.2 trillion.[11] This is a *tripling* of value over the last twenty years: in 2003, the total value was $14.2 trillion.

The Growth of Billionaire Wealth Since 2003

Total U.S. billionaire wealth, 2003 to 2023

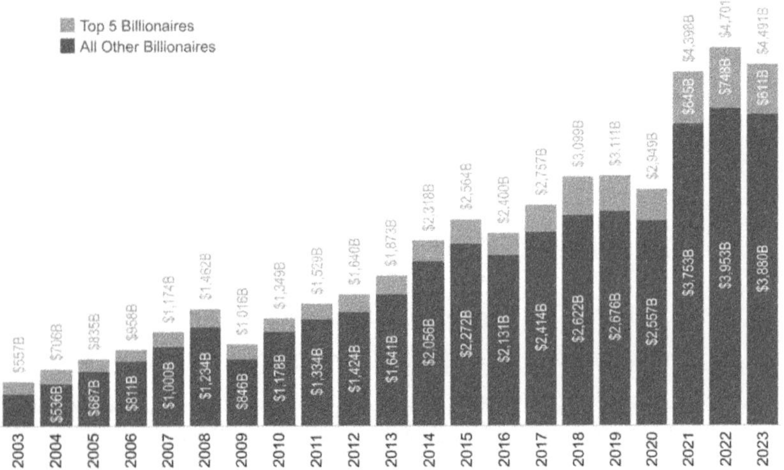

Source: *Forbes*' Real-Time Billionaires List.

Growing Share of Stock Market Wealth Is Owned by the Richest 1 Percent

Share of stock and mutual funds owned by U.S. households in different wealth brackets, 2002–2023

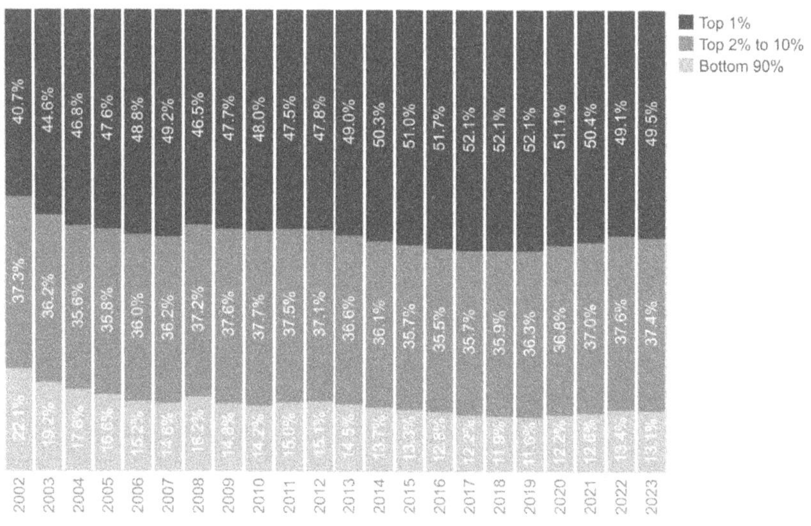

St. Louis Federal Reserve, share of corporate equities and mutual fund shares by households at selected wealth levels.

A 2023 analysis of stock markets by the Federal Reserve found that the concentration of ownership of the public equity stock market is at an all-time high, with the richest 10 percent of the population owning a staggering 93 percent of stock market wealth.[12] As Irina Ivanova wrote in *Fortune* magazine, "The running of the bulls in 2023 was more like the waddle of the fat cats."[13] The lion's share of these gains went to the richest 1 percent, who own 54 percent of public equity markets, up from 40 percent in 2002, according to Fed data.[14] The next 9 percent (or households in the ninetieth to ninety-ninth percentile) saw their share of public market value grow from 38 percent in 2002 to 39 percent, a modest gain.[15] For comparison's sake, total stock market wealth is now roughly equal to the $47 trillion value of all U.S. residential real estate, according to Redfin.[16]

There's been a lot of chatter about the "democratization" of public equity markets, with a growing percentage of the population becoming investors.[17] The Fed estimates that 58 percent of U.S. households have some money in the stock market, mostly through retirement funds like IRAs and mutual funds.[18] But the more telling statistic is that it is the top 1 percent of American wealth holders who own fully half of the stock market. The bottom 90 percent of Americans own a paltry 7 percent of stock market value, with the lower 50 percent of earners owning a mere 1 percent. The key trend: a continuing concentration of stock market wealth. As Gillian Tett observed in the *Financial Times,* "If nothing else, these rising concentrations merit far more public debate, since they challenge America's self-image of its political economy and financial democracy."[19]

These graphs are evidence that we are living in a plutocratic economy, where the rules are tipped in favor of the billionaires at the expense of everyone else. Furthermore, among the superrich, trends are shifting away from entrepreneurial wealth to inherited wealth dynasties. A 2023 UBS study found that new billionaires are more likely to have inherited their wealth rather than building it through a family enterprise.[20]

A huge intergenerational wealth transfer is underway, with an estimated $105 trillion flowing from the baby boomers, born between 1946 and 1964, to Gen Xers and millennials. More than half the inheritances, an estimated $62 trillion,

The Rich Own Stock, the Bottom 90 Percent Hold Debt

Share of U.S. assets and debt by income level, Q4 2023

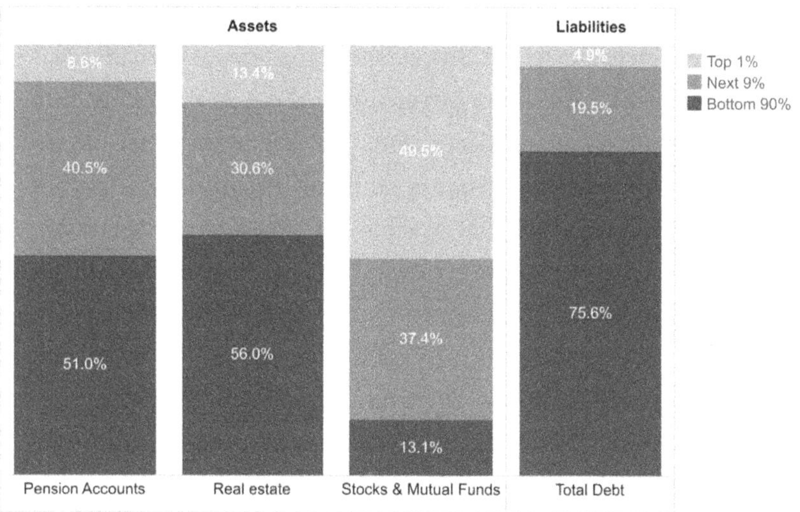

Source: Distributional financial accounts data from the U.S. Federal Reserve.

will flow from very wealthy households in the top 2 percent. Only one in five households will receive any of this wealth transfer, according to the analysis conducted by Cerulli Associates.[21]

As we discussed in chapter 2, as billionaires move from the accumulation phase of wealth generation, their focus becomes using their power to defend and preserve that wealth, including influencing tax and social policy by capturing political systems. This is one of the harms of a society plagued by excessive wealth. Such societies with growing dynastic wealth are unfriendly to citizens who don't already have wealth, because there is a breakdown in social solidarity ("we're all in the same boat") and a reluctance by wealthy households to pay taxes toward investments in public programs that foster opportunity, like debt-free education, early childhood health, and higher minimum wages.

In sum, the social mobility that Americans enjoyed during the post–World War II era has stalled out. The American Dream has moved to Canada. Yes: if you are not born in Affluent Town or Richistan but aspire to the American Dream of owning a home, retiring before you die, and a better life for your children, you are better off living in Canada or countries in northern Europe that now have much greater social mobility than does the United States. Why? Because these countries make government investments in early childhood education, broad access to health care, debt-free higher education, and job and skills training—all drivers of economic mobility.

The other reason why the American Dream has diminished is the greed of the billionaire titans of industry and owners of capital, who are hoarding an ever-greater share of the fruits of the American economy for themselves.

Excessive wealth at the top of the heap infects and diminishes the well-being of the rest of society below it, by depressing wages, shifting the tax burden from those who can afford to pay more to the regular Joes, and shrinking the ability of government to invest in services and education that would power the economic mobility of the whole of society. A segment of the billionaire class and their advocates promote a strategic deflection, encouraging working-class people to focus their resentments on recent immigrants as the reason for their economic precarity. Meanwhile, billionaires and their minions labor to deflect the public's gaze away from their primary role in siphoning an ever-greater share of the profits of the economy into their own pockets, through both wage suppression and the flexing of their political power to rig the rules of the game.

"Oligarchy"—rule by the few—and "plutocracy"—rule by the wealthy—are technically accurate terms for our state of growing inequality and concentration of power, but they don't fully capture how billionaire domination thoroughly infects and diminishes the health of an entire society. The better term, I believe, is "billionaire disruption." We are being burned by billionaires.

Part Two

THE BILLIONAIRE BURN

How the Wealth of a Few Impoverishes the Many

Our society has been undergoing a slow march toward oligarchy, with billionaires exercising ever-greater power and influence to shape the world in their interests.

The lives of the rich and the ordinary American have become further divergent, as the environs of the wealthy become ever more luxurious, while the economic status of the middle class becomes more precarious. The reality is that the United States is "polarizing and its social arteries hardening," wrote Will Hutton, a British observer of U.S. society. "The sumptuousness and bleakness of the respective lifestyles of rich and poor represent a scale of difference and opportunity that is almost medieval—and a standing offense to the American expectation that everyone has the opportunity for life, liberty and happiness."[1]

Economist John Kenneth Galbraith described it best as "public squalor and private luxury," one that undermines the commonweal and reorients an entire society to service the billionaire class.

Concentrated wealth is warping virtually every dimension of our daily lives: where we get our news and entertainment, how much we pay to park our cars, and the cost of our groceries. The chapters in this section examine the ways the billionaire class directly diminishes your life—from your health, your pocketbook, and your housing options to the quality of the environment and more.

CHAPTER 4

BILLIONAIRES ARE TRASHING THE PLANET

THE GLOBAL BILLIONAIRE CLASS IS DISPROPORTIONATELY degrading our one and only common resource: Planet Earth—the water, soil, forests, and atmosphere that sustain all life. This is the result of their unsustainable levels of consumption, but also the exercise of significant political power to block environmental protections and push for further fossil fuel extraction. In addition to propelling us toward climate catastrophe, this overconsumption is depleting sources of fresh water, exposing us to toxins, acidifying our oceans, and contributing to the extinction of hundreds of species of plants, insects, and animals.[1]

For humanity and other species to survive, the rich will have to change their behavior to a much greater degree than everyone else. Unfortunately, the billionaires and their industry lobbyists are pressing for pathways that require no change in their profligate consumption.

YOUR CARBON FOOTPRINT VERSUS THE BIG SHOES OF BILLIONAIRES

The annual carbon footprint of the average U.S. resident (including billionaires) is about 16 tons of emissions per year.

(The global average footprint is considerably smaller, about 4 tons per person.)[2] But carbon emissions from the wealthiest people are much, much greater. One study found that twenty billionaires in the sample were responsible for an annual average of about 8,190 tons of greenhouse gas emissions, with some emitting far more. The wealthiest 1 percent globally, roughly 77 million people, emit 16 percent of the world's CO_2 emissions—more than the bottom two-thirds of humanity, more than 5 billion people combined. The richest 10 percent account for half of global emissions.[3]

Since the 1990s, the richest 1 percent have used up twice as much of the carbon we had left to burn without increasing global temperatures above the 1.5°C (2.7°F) safe limit, a planetary threshold that we may have blown past in 2024.[4] These wealthy emitters burn an average of 110 tons of carbon each year. The emissions of the top 1 percent will cause 1.3 million excess deaths due to heat between 2020 and 2030, according to an Oxfam report drawing on research from the Stockholm Environmental Institute.[5] This über-wealthy class is driving an unsustainable level of consumption, contributing to not only climate change but the extraction of minerals, consumption of water, and dumping of plastics into the environment.

It is the billionaires, however, who do the lion's share of damage.

For example, Larry Ellison, co-founder of the software giant Oracle, who is worth $210.5 billion according to *Forbes*, has an annual carbon consumption footprint of 6,936 tons, hundreds of times greater than that of the average American.[6] This is in large part due to Ellison's superyacht, which includes

Billionaire Emissions

Tons of carbon dioxide emitted by the homes, boats, planes, and other vehicles

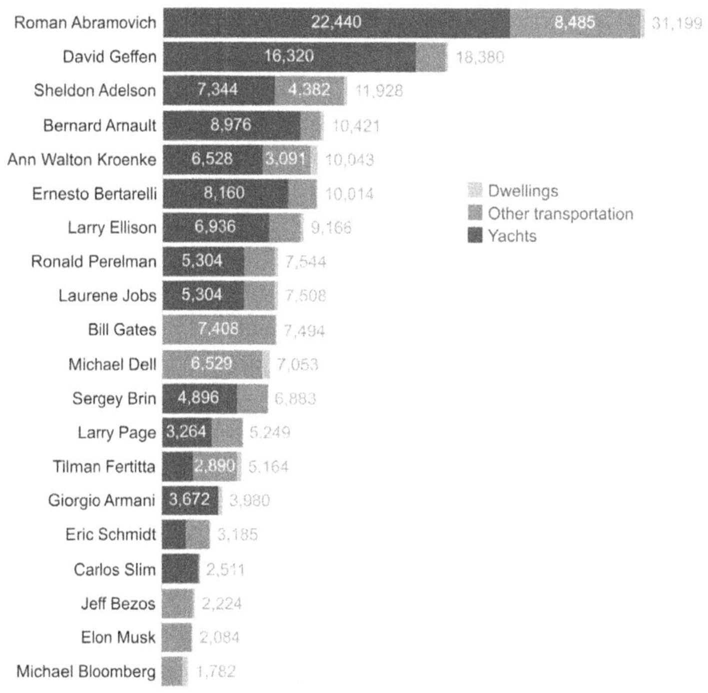

Source: "Private planes, mansions and superyachts: What gives billionaires like Musk and Abramovich such a massive carbon footprint," Richard Wilk and Beatriz Barros, *The Conversation*, February 16, 2021. Other transportation includes planes, helicopters, and cars.

a helicopter pad, submarines, and a pool.[7] According to one assessment, 125 of the richest billionaires invest so much in polluting companies that they are responsible for emitting an average of 3 million tons of carbon a year.[8]

Russian oligarch Roman Abramovich, a billionaire oil and gas trader who until recently owned London's Chelsea Football

Club, is worth an estimated $9.7 billion.[9] He has a 533-foot yacht, the *Eclipse,* the second largest in the world, that also includes a submarine. He flies on two private jets, a Boeing 767 with a thirty-seat dining room, and a Gulfstream G650, for shorter hops, along with two helicopters. Like many billionaires, he has mansions around the world, including a fifteen-bedroom mansion in London's Kensington Park, a home in Israel, a château in Cap d'Antibes in France, and a seventy-acre compound in St. Barts.[10] By one estimate, Abramovich was responsible for 33,859 metric tons of CO_2 emissions in 2018.[11]

Microsoft founder Bill Gates is responsible for a lot of emissions from his private jet and sprawling mansions. Gates doesn't own a yacht, but he does quite a bit of private jet travel. Flying on a private jet creates ten to twenty times more emissions per passenger than commercial flying. His massive estate, Xanadu, in Medina, Washington, covers 6,131 square meters. Gates owns additional homes in Palm Springs, California, and New York City, a horse farm in Wellington, Florida,[12] four private jets, a seaplane, and a bevy of helicopters.[13] Owning multiple homes and properties over several time zones consumes huge amounts of energy, water, and other resources. By one estimate, Gates has an annual carbon footprint of 7,493 metric tons.

AN ELYSIUM FUTURE

If you want to visualize how billionaires may dominate our future and environment, Hollywood has already imagined it for you: the 2013 blockbuster science fiction film, *Elysium,* starring Matt Damon and Jodie Foster, is set in a dystopian

Los Angeles of 2154, degraded by ecological disasters and extreme inequalities of wealth.

In the film, the billionaire class have relocated to the ultimate gated community, a pristine orbital space station called Elysium. (Director Neill Blomkamp did location shots for the film in Malibu, California, replete with turquoise swimming pools and palatial mansions.)[14] On Elysium, most physical illnesses are cured by climbing into a "med-bay," a contraption that looks like a designer MRI machine. As a result, life expectancy is three times longer on Elysium than on contaminated Earth.

The film's scenes of Earth, by contrast, were filmed in a populated garbage dump in Mexico City. On Earth, life is toxic, brutal, and short. People dream of getting to Elysium to cure their cancers and other environmental illnesses. Damon's character, Max Da Costa, is exposed to a lethal dose of radiation, and his only chance of survival is to get to Elysium.

Elysium is a dire depiction of our society's extreme inequalities of wealth. The film's amusing website, www.itsbetterup-there.com, included advertisements for fictional enterprises such as "Elysium Realty," with slogans including "Live Above It All," and "It's Better Up There," with home prices starting at $250 million.[15]

Unfortunately, there is a lot about this depiction that is resonant with our current reality. Like the residents of Elysium, today's billionaires often live in buffered enclaves, far from corners of the Earth degraded by their overconsumption of natural resources and investments in extractive industries. The excessively wealthy often have multiple properties around the world, so if one home is threatened by fire, flood, or extreme heat, they can always jet to a less affected corner.

Meanwhile, most of humanity—those without the means to protect themselves—struggles to survive from a problem largely created by others living far away. According to Oxfam, more than 91 percent of deaths caused by climate-related disasters over the last fifty years occurred in low-income countries with the lowest carbon footprints in the world. Death from flooding is seven times greater in countries such as Bangladesh and regions like West Africa than in the big carbon-emitting countries.[16]

Because of their distance and disconnection from pollution, the excessively wealthy may be the last to wake up to the personal consequences of a warming planet. Some, more cynically, are perfectly aware of our ecological peril but, rather than restrict their profligate consumption, choose instead to invest in individualistic solutions such as Elysium-like gated communities, bunkers, and resilient enclaves to ride out future disruptions.[17] Another handful of the very wealthiest billionaires, most notably, Elon Musk, Jeff Bezos, and Richard Branson, are literally investing in "Plan B" space travel to colonies on Mars, to which most of humanity will not be invited.

Even the luxury "swanktuaries"—the high-end homes and condos built to park wealth (described further in chapter 6)—siphon resources from other more useful infrastructure projects. Across major global cities, towers of excess are rising, many of them sparsely occupied monuments to vanity that waste construction materials and human labor that could have been deployed to build sorely needed affordable housing. One luxury apartment building in Boston, One Dalton Place, required extension of a fracked-gas pipeline to serve a largely empty building with gas ignition fireplaces and heated swimming pools.[18]

BILLIONAIRES NEED TO CHANGE THEIR BEHAVIOR FIRST

Globally, there are a handful of countries that are the biggest drivers of climate disruption and environmental degradation. With roughly 4.4 percent of the world's population, the United States has historically consumed a huge percentage of the planet's natural resources, with some estimates as high as 35 percent.[19] And within wealthy countries like the United States, mega-wealthy consumers set the pace as the drivers and cultural exemplars of profligacy.

To limit global warming from blowing past the 1.5°C (2.7°F) tipping point of disastrous no return, each person on the planet must reduce their annual carbon emissions to below 1 ton of carbon. Overall, we needed to have cut global emissions by 48 percent by 2023 to avert the worst climate disasters. In part because of billionaire consumption and protection of the fossil fuel and other high-pollutant industries, we have failed to reach this goal, with dire prospects for all our futures.

Indeed, as our societies work to transition away from fossil fuels, the emissions of the richest 1 percent across the globe are canceling out these efforts. Instead of "carbon offsets"—activities that reduce emissions in the atmosphere—billionaire behaviors are effectively "carbon bombs." *The carbon emissions of billionaires alone cancel out the benefits of approximately 1 million wind turbines every year.* To put that in perspective, it has taken the United States more than four decades to install almost eighty thousand wind turbines.[20]

An inescapable conclusion is that the billionaire class must make the largest adjustments in their behavior in order to reduce emissions. Low-income people, especially those living in regions that produce the least in per capita emissions, should not be required to make sacrifices before the wealthiest people on the globe do more to reduce their excessive lifestyles.

PRIVATE JET EXCESS

Most billionaires own private jets; some even own multiple luxury aircraft. The average private jet owner has an estimated wealth of $190 million (the average fractional jet owner in businesses like NetJets is worth $140 million), according to Wealth-X.[21] As more and more billionaires emerge from the growing thicket of inequality, demand for private jets has skyrocketed (pun intended), especially as the commercial flying experience becomes more degrading. Today, there are more than 26,000 private luxury jets in use in the world, with two-thirds of them based in the United States. Private jet emissions surged 46 percent between 2019 and 2023.[22]

At S&P 500 corporations, private jet use has increased 35 percent since 2019. In 2022 alone, Meta, the big tech company that owns Facebook and Instagram, spent $6.6 million in private jets for CEO Mark Zuckerberg and his former COO Sheryl Sandberg alone.[23] A 2023 survey of global companies found that 85 percent of them have no plans to reduce their business air travel emissions.[24]

These jets not only emit millions of tons of carbon each year, but also don't contribute a fair share toward the collective infrastructure costs of air travel. Private aviation, including private jets, accounts for 16 percent of U.S. air traffic but chips in only 2 percent of the costs of operating the airspace.[25]

Private plane manufacturers and owners would like us to believe a private jet is a necessary business tool in a fast-paced global economy. But an in-depth analysis of private jet use at Hanscom Field, New England's largest private jet airport, found that more than half the flights are used for travel to luxury recreation destinations, like Aspen, Barcelona, Jackson Hole, and West Palm Beach. And many were short-hop flights from New York City to places like Nantucket, Martha's Vineyard, and the Hamptons of eastern Long Island, destinations with excellent transportation alternatives to private jet travel.[26]

Seven of the top twenty private jets traveling in and out of Hanscom Field are owned by individuals and shell companies affiliated with billionaire-owned private equity firms. Over the year and a half of air travel studied, these twenty jets alone took more than 3,240 flights and were responsible for an

"I try to do my part."

estimated 14,930 tons of emissions. The most frequent flyer took 112 trips from Hanscom Field in suburban Boston to Nantucket Island, a ninety-one-mile short-hop destination served by more carbon-friendly options like high-speed ferries and electric-powered small aircraft.[27]

Limiting luxury travel consumption seems like low-hanging fruit for reducing emissions. Unfortunately, we are talking about limiting the behavior of billionaires, the wealthiest and most powerful people on the planet, who won't countenance the notion of flying with the masses—or, God forbid, taking the train. States, localities, and activists should oppose expansion of private jet airport facilities just as much as they oppose the building of new fossil fuel pipelines. Happily, a proposal to triple the capacity for private jets at Hanscom Field outside Boston has roused significant opposition for this very reason.[28]

The private jet lobby would like us to believe that in a few short years, they will have transitioned their sector away from kerosene-based jet fuels to sustainable aviation fuels. Research I coauthored found that there is currently no realistic or scalable alternative to fossil-fuel kerosene that would power current aviation needs, let alone projections of future growth.[29]

YACHT EXCESS

Private jets are indefensible on a warming planet. But aside from the private space travel being indulged by Elon Musk and Jeff Bezos, the most ecologically damaging form of luxury transport is far and away the superyacht. Business leaders may argue that jets are a necessary form of transportation for busy executives, but nobody *needs* a superyacht.

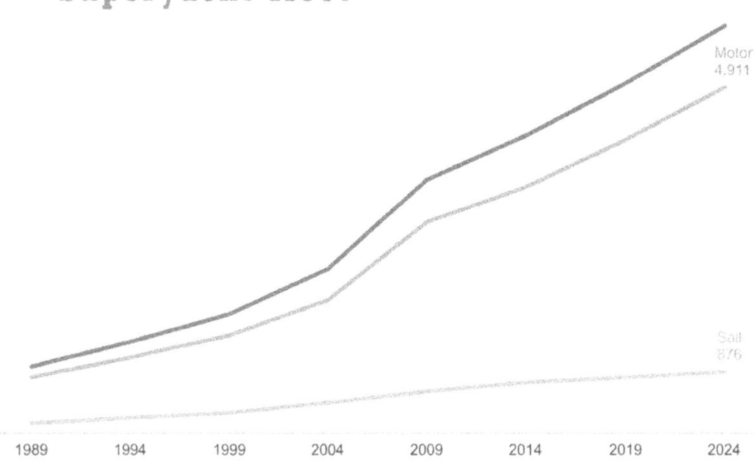

Source: "The State of Yachting 2024," *Superyacht Times*, March 28, 2024.

The new breed of even bigger superyachts, boats with a length overall of more than two hundred feet, indulge the unbridled pleasure and vanity of the billionaire class, as symbols of wealth, power, and competitive ostentation. The demand for superyachts has risen along with the growth of the billionaire class over the last few decades. Francesca Webster, editor of the trade magazine *Superyacht Times,* described for a BBC reporter in 2024 an unprecedented and "massive spike in new build and used yacht purchases."[30] Since 2006, the global fleet of superyachts has exploded from 3,000 to 5,787 boats.[31]

As inequality grows, so does the length of the yachts. Within the rarified world of the extremely wealthy, there are the "haves and have yachts," with additional stratification among yacht owners. As journalist Evan Osnos observed in a lengthy and jaw-dropping article in the *New Yorker,* "A big ship is a floating manse, with a hierarchy written right into the nomenclature." In the yacht society, yachts are generally identified in quatrains indicative of the source, extent, and breadth of their owners' wealth:

* Luxury goods mogul Bernard Arnault: $202.1 billion. Superyacht: 333-foot *Symphony*.

* Dallas Cowboys owner Jerry Jones: $14.4 billion. Superyacht: 358-foot *Bravo Eugenia*.

* Miriam Adelson, widow of casino magnate Sheldon Adelson: $29.8 billion. Superyacht: 300-foot *Queen Miri*.

Yachts are the most expensive luxury item among billionaire holdings. A billionaire might spend $50 million to $100 million on a private jet. To date, the most expensive residence ever sold in the United States was a $240 million quadplex on Central Park, to hedge fund investor Ken Griffin. But many superyachts can soak up even greater piles of cash, regularly exceeding $250 million to construct, and with another one-tenth of the purchase price in annual maintenance costs.[32]

On these floating mansions, the amenities are other-worldly: glass elevators, IMAX theaters, all-teak wood decks, hospital equipment capable of testing for pathogens, "infinite wine cellars," freshwater swimming pools, penthouse apartments on upper decks, basketball courts, glass-walled observation rooms, museum-level art, Turkish baths, and even ski rooms where guests can suit up before being helicoptered to a ski resort on the mainland.

The ultimate yacht accessory is . . . another yacht! Billionaire Jan Koum, founder of WhatsApp ($15.9 billion), owns

Moonrise, a 327-foot yacht that cost $220 million. Koum also owns a companion yacht, the 224-foot *Nebula,* which cost $40 million. Today, having a dedicated "service vessel" is a growing trend among the very wealthiest superyacht owners, to carry additional amenities, like an air-conditioned helicopter hanger.[33]

The superyacht elites can be seen passing New Year's Eve on St. Barts, then motoring to the Palm Beach International Boat Show in March, where they show off their gleaming swanktuaries upon the seas to other wealthy billionaires. In May, the superyachts gather in Venice for the World Superyacht Awards, about as close as the planet gets to a billionaire phallic competition. By September, the superyachts have sailed to the tax haven of Monaco for the Monaco Yacht Show, what the *Daily Mail* calls the "most shamelessly ostentatious

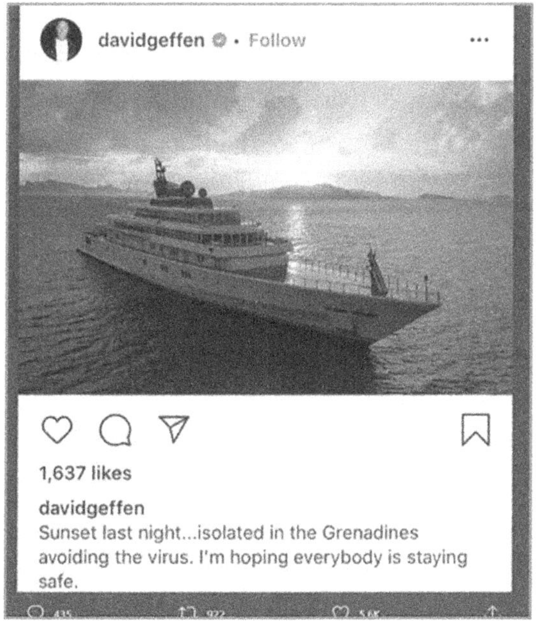
davidgeffen • Follow
1,637 likes
davidgeffen
Sunset last night...isolated in the Grenadines avoiding the virus. I'm hoping everybody is staying safe.

display of yachts in the world."[34] Monaco is the favored venue in which to ride out the Caribbean hurricane season, one of the several supercharged weather events fueled by the disproportionate emissions of said yachts.

Former music and film mogul David Geffen ($8.1 billion), co-founder of DreamWorks, owns a 454-foot, eighty-two-room monstrosity called *The Rising Sun*. Early in the COVID pandemic, he Instagrammed a photo of his yacht, captioned "Sunset last night . . . isolated in the Grenadines avoiding the virus. I'm hoping everybody is staying safe."[35] Maybe Geffen should rename his yacht *The Clueless*.

The average diesel-powered superyacht produces about as much annual carbon emissions as 1,500 passenger vehicles.[36] Geffen's superyacht emits 16,320 tons of greenhouse gases every year, almost eight hundred times what the average American emits in a year, according to researchers Beatriz Barros and Richard Wilk.[37] Multiply this offense by the almost six thousand supersize vessels that exceed the ninety-eight-foot standard definition of a superyacht.[38] Journalist Joe Fassler reports that a two-hundred-foot yacht slurps up 132 gallons of diesel fuel *an hour* and burns through 2,200 gallons to travel a distance of one hundred nautical miles. This private fleet of floating playgrounds, observes Fassler, "pollutes as much as entire nations: The 300 biggest boats alone emit 315,000 tons of carbon dioxide each year—about as much as Burundi's more than 10 million inhabitants."[39]

In addition to being huge consumers of diesel fuel and contributors to climate change, the superyachts have additional harmful environmental impacts. The nautical toys of billionaires contribute to other forms of marine pollution, including ocean acidification, noise, toxins, and plastic waste.

As Joe Fassler writes, "If we're serious about avoiding climate chaos, we need to tax, or at the very least shame, these resource-hoarding behemoths out of existence. In fact, taking on the carbon aristocracy, and their most emissions-intensive modes of travel and leisure, may be the best chance we have to improve our collective climate morale and increase our appetite for personal sacrifice, from individual behavior changes to sweeping policy mandates."

Lobbyists for the private jet and superyacht industries will wax on about the jobs created in both building and operating these fleets (and in truth, the typical yacht has many more people staffing the craft than guests on board). But there are even more jobs in building and operating mass transit and other public and private green infrastructure. The human and natural resources diverted from life-affirming and energy-efficient investments is one of the massive opportunity costs of billionaire extravagance.

CLIMATE CRIMINALS

You may be thinking, "Hey, aren't we all responsible for climate change and changing our behavior?" Of course we all need to take responsibility for reducing our energy consumption, especially those of us who live in advanced industrialized nations that have been burning oil for a century. But not all contributions to climate disruption are equal: Some take the bus while others fly private jets. And some people have considerably more political power and wealth to influence the paths we have taken or, regrettably, not taken.

We cannot ignore the powerful decision-makers and mega-consumers among a segment of the wealthy that have locked us onto a destructive trajectory that condemns us all to a bleak future. These people therefore bear disproportionate responsibility.

The problem here is not just excess consumption, which is significant. For that, a democratic society could levy consumption taxes and legislate constraints. The real problem is the *power* that these ultra-wealthy households wield to fend off regulation of fossil fuel–burning corporations that they own and invest in. A 2022 Oxfam analysis found that the fossil fuel investments of 125 billionaires emitted, on average, 3 million tons of CO_2 each year. This is more than 1 million times more than an average person in the bottom 90 percent of global wealth households.[40] "With their heavy influence over the media, politics, and policy makers, the super-rich are able to protect their financial interests by stopping any progress made toward transitioning to renewable energy," said Oxfam in their 2023 report, *Climate Equality: A Planet for the 99%*.[41]

Among the billionaires are the "carbon barons," the considerable family fortunes that come from oil, gas, and coal—with a few "methane barons" in the mix as well. With few exceptions, these ultra-wealthy families, along with the corporations and foundations they control, have deployed their considerable clout to fund sham science and climate change denial, block green alternatives, and delay global responses aimed at reducing emissions. These industries, which in recent years have cynically claimed they are leading the way toward "net zero emissions," are spending trillions on new fossil fuel extraction infrastructure under the assumption that governments will not be able to stop them. In other words, they are running out humanity's clock.[42]

Imagine a time, in the not-too-distant future, when an international tribunal convenes to ask the question: Who is responsible for climate disruption? Who knew about the dangers of burning oil, gas, and coal, with its atmosphere-altering properties, but did nothing about it? Or worse, which individuals worked to fund and promote disinformation, block changes, and delay action?

We now know that certain corporations, like ExxonMobil and Shell, hold oversize responsibility for limiting our present options.[43] There are individuals presiding over these powerful transnational institutions who wield the clout of medium-size nation-states. These are the "apex predators" in the climate *inaction* ecosystem. Future generations will know their names: they are the climate criminals.

The Climate Accountability Research Project has identified twenty-four "Climate Criminals" most responsible for—and most enriched by—preventing action to mitigate fossil fuel production and consumption. Their combined wealth is at least $29.8 billion, with an average of $1.7 billion. Here are profiles of three billionaires of this group:[44]

Kelcy Warren (worth $7.7 billion) is the billionaire chairman of Energy Transfer, the company behind the Dakota Access Pipeline. His alleged climate crimes include his company's ecologically destructive pipelines and dangerous hazardous spills, filing lawsuits against environmental groups and anti-pipeline protestors in attempts to silence opposition, and hiring a military contractor to infiltrate groups of peaceful protestors.[45]

Jamie Dimon ($2.6 billion). Since the 2015 Paris Agreement, the global compact to reduce greenhouse gas emissions, JPMorgan

Chase has funneled $434 billion in investment funds to the fossil fuel industry under the leadership of its CEO, Jamie Dimon.[46] Not only is JPMorgan the largest bank in the United States, but it's also the largest single financier of fossil fuels and one of the top six financiers of natural gas fracking.[47] JPMorgan has invested in eight power plants in the Philippines and in fracking projects in Argentina and has financed the Mountain Valley Pipeline, a controversial three-hundred-mile pipeline that would traverse waterways and federal forest lands on its path between West Virginia and Virginia.[48]

Harold Hamm ($18.5 billion). "America's richest oil man" organized quid pro quo campaign financing deals between Big Oil executives and Donald Trump to leading Continental Resources, one of the largest companies producing oil and fracking natural gas in the United States. He also leads the Domestic Energy Producers Alliance, a group with the goal to "produce more American oil and natural gas."[49] Hamm was a convenor of fossil fuel billionaires who offered to raise millions for Donald Trump's second-term agenda of rolling back climate protection legislation.[50]

Many ultra-wealthy people believe they will be able to maintain their luxurious lifestyle and unsustainable levels of consumption as we transition to a greener economy. As Emma Garnett and Charlotte A. Kukowski write, "With the ability to successfully lobby against climate policies, the super-wealthy have no compulsion to curb their highly polluting behavior. For example, private jet travel remains legal despite it being the most polluting transport mode of all and useful to just a tiny minority."[51]

They promote the illusion that we will unplug the carbon-emitting fossil fuel sources and plug in green energy sources, enabling them to continue roaring on and jetting about the globe. And while the transition to green energy is promising, our societies will still need to dramatically reduce consumption of all the natural resource inputs that power our modern lifestyle. In short, the wealthy will need to reduce their consumption and change their behaviors, alongside but to a greater degree than everyone else.

THE PERILS OF UNEQUAL SACRIFICE

Possibly the biggest harm caused by billionaire environmental excess is that it undermines the culture of *shared sacrifice* that will be required to effectively reduce greenhouse gas emissions.

After it was revealed that influencer Kylie Jenner took a seventeen-minute private jet flight between two L.A.-area airports, one Twitter user quipped sardonically: "kylie jenner is out here taking 3-minute flights with her private jet, but I'm the one who has to use paper straws."

As journalist Joe Fassler writes, "Whether we're talking about voluntary changes (insulating our attics and taking public transit) or mandated ones (tolerating a wind farm on the horizon or saying goodbye to a lush lawn), the climate fight hinges, to some extent, on our willingness to participate. When the ultra-rich are given a free pass, we lose faith in the value of that sacrifice."[52] Fassler continues, "In that sense, super polluting yachts and jets don't just worsen climate change; they lessen the chance that we will work together to fix it. Why bother when the luxury goods mogul Bernard Arnault is cruising around on the Symphony, a $150 million, 333-foot superyacht?"

Fassler cites the research of cognitive scientists Nicolas Baumard and Coralie Chevallier, who observe that people "stop cooperating when they see that some people are not doing their part." Most people are aware of the harms caused by the excessive consumption of oil, coal, and gas, though they may not know the full extent of the billionaires' share. But if one's neighbors aren't altering their behavior, it's hard to

"We'll begin boarding our first-class passengers after a ten-minute pause in honor of the even wealthier people who fly in private jets."

bind together and build a movement that will require shared sacrifice. And if the billionaires are consuming with abandon, it's hard not to feel like a chump for making different choices.

"If some people are allowed to emit 10 times as much carbon for their comfort," Mr. Baumard and Ms. Chevallier ask in an op-ed in *Le Monde,* "then why restrict your meat consumption, turn down your thermostat or limit your purchases of new products?"[53]

Similarly, why would low-emitting countries agree to emission reductions when U.S. billionaires are not altering their behavior and are lobbying to withdraw from global compacts?

If you believe, as I do, that we are facing an ecologically and economically disrupted future, then this breakdown of solidarity has real consequences. And the reverse is also true if we can reduce billionaire wealth and broaden wealth and well-being. As Richard Wilkinson and Kate Pickett, authors of the book *The Spirit Level: Why Greater Equality Makes Societies Stronger,* write in a 2024 magazine article, "Greater equality will reduce unhealthy and excess consumption, and will increase the solidarity and cohesion that are needed to make societies more adaptable in the face of climate and other emergencies."[54] Reduced wealth concentration and consumption are the preconditions we need to be prepared for whatever future comes our way.

CHAPTER 5

BILLIONAIRES ARE MAKING YOU PAY HIGHER TAXES

THE BILLIONAIRES ARE HAPPY FOR YOU TO PAY MORE taxes so they can pay less.

Billionaires are using their political influence and legal prowess to reduce their own taxes. They thereby shift onto you the responsibility of paying for public services of every stripe: from caring for veterans and protecting national parks to building roads and repairing bridges and shielding the public from infectious diseases. While most people understand that taxes are the price we pay for a healthy and orderly society, we ought to be offended by having to pay more in order to pick up the tab of billionaires.

Tax avoidance is just one of many ways that billionaires rig the rules. The rest of us are also subsidizing their lavish lifestyles with tax breaks and subsidies, like the "mansion subsidy" (the home mortgage interest deduction) in which 17 percent of the subsidy goes to the top 1 percent of households.[1] Commercial flyers and taxpayers basically subsidize the luxury jet-setters, who do not pay their fair share of the cost of a regulated airspace.[2]

Meanwhile, many lobbyists for the super-wealthy push for spending cuts to public investments and services that help foster opportunity, promote social mobility, and backstop decent lives for the non-rich.

FIFTY YEARS OF TAX SHIFTING

If we want to "unrig" an economy that favors billionaires at the expense of everyone else, we need to start with the tax code. Over the last fifty years, the super-wealthy and their lobbyists have worked successfully to shift taxes off themselves and onto everyone else. There are multiple shifts underway, what we could call "shift, shrink, and shaft."

As this chapter will show, over the last half century, federal and state lawmakers in the United States have approved four significant shifts of taxation:

* off higher-income and wealthy taxpayers and onto non-wealthy taxpayers
* off taxes on income from assets and onto taxes on wages (i.e., taxing work, not wealth)
* off global corporations and onto individual taxpayers
* off the federal tax system, which is more progressive, and onto state and local tax systems, which are more regressive

A lot of what we know about abuses of the tax code and the shocking levels of tax avoidance by the wealthy comes from leaked data. Over the last fifteen years, the International

Consortium of Investigative Journalists has obtained massive amounts of data from people inside the wealth defense industry—lawyers, wealth managers, and financial advisers. The consortium has verified these leaks and organized them into massive folios such as the Panama Papers in 2016 and the Pandora Papers in 2021.[3] The independent journalism outfit ProPublica obtained a tranche of leaked IRS data that it has published as "The Secret IRS Files."[4] These disclosures reveal the various aggressive methods the wealthy use to avoid taxes.

Shift: Tax Cuts for Billionaires

The ProPublica "tax secrets" research found that many billionaires, including Jeff Bezos, Michael Bloomberg, and Elon Musk, have in many years paid *zero* income taxes. Zero. Between 2014 and 2018, another twenty-five billionaires saw their combined wealth increase $401 billion, yet paid an effective income tax rate of 3.4 percent. During this same period, the median U.S. household earned about $70,000 in income and paid an effective federal tax rate of 14 percent.[5]

If the tax code wasn't already sufficiently rigged in favor of the billionaires, in 2017 Congress passed the Tax Cuts and Jobs Act, commonly known as the "Trump Tax Cuts." Many of the costliest provisions that reduced government revenue were additional windfall tax reductions for billionaires.

For example, the Tax Cuts and Jobs Act increased the wealth exemption of the estate and gift tax, the only U.S. tax levied solely on the inherited wealth of multimillionaires and billionaires. Specifically, it doubled the amount of wealth exempted from $6.8 million for an individual to $13.99 million in 2025 ($27.98 million for a couple), adjusted for inflation on an annual basis. In other words, today no one with inherited wealth below $14 million (or a couple with $28 million) will pay *any* estate tax.[6] That means a wealthy couple can pass $25 million onto their kids without a penny of it being taxed by the federal government (and only sixteen states and the District of Columbia levy estate or inheritance taxes).[7]

The 2017 Trump tax cut legislation also created a new loophole, called a "pass through deduction," for business income, which gives preferential tax treatment to income flowing through so-called chapter S corporations.[8] The new provision, known as Section 199A, is an arbitrary determination that income from certain types of businesses should be treated more favorably than wages from workers and other types of businesses. Law professor Daniel Shaviro of New York University described this new rule as the "worst provision ever even to be proposed in the history of the federal income tax."[9]

At a May 2018 gathering of financial advisers to the wealthy, only a few months after passage of the Trump tax cut, the attendees were trilling with excitement about the new tax-dodging possibilities presented by the change in law. One wealth defense planner told the conference that the Section 199A provision "leaves a gaping hole in the tax code." He stated, "The goal by the end of the presentation today is to make you guys the bus drivers, or the truck drivers, to drive right through that hole with your clients."[10] And indeed they have.

Billionaires and CEOs have used the S corp provision to game their tax liability down significantly. According to ProPublica, the owner and CEO of WeatherTech floor mats, David MacNeil, dropped his taxable income from $68 million in 2017 to $47 million in 2018 using the pass-through loophole. Jeffrey Records, CEO of MidFirst Bank in Oklahoma, dropped his taxable salary from $8.6 million to $1.8 million. Dick Uihlein, chairman of Uline, gamed his taxable income down to $2.1 million from $5.1 million.[11]

Shift: Taxing Work, Not Wealth

A good place to start unrigging the tax code would be the laws that give tax preference to wealth and assets over work and wages. Right now, income from long-term capital gains is taxed at 15 or 20 percent, while the top tax rate on wage income over $609,000 is 37 percent. A simple fix is to tax income over a certain level at the same rate, regardless of its source. For example, income over $1 million, whether from wages, wealth, or inheritance, could be taxed at the different graduated rates currently levied on wage income.

The key is to end the preferential treatment of income from investments and inheritances. Lawmakers should enact a new tax code that more fairly distributes the gains of a modern economy to the working people who made this productivity possible. At the same time, our tax code should require that those who have disproportionately benefited from U.S. economic prosperity be taxed to make investments creating broad opportunity for others, such as making higher education affordable, rather than allowing them to amass concentrations of wealth that skew our democracy. The Patriotic Millionaires, a group of wealthy Americans advocating for progressive tax reform, have put forward just such a program in their report, *Crack the Code 2.0: Proposed Internal Revenue Code of 2026*.[12]

Shift: Taxing Individuals, Not Big Corporations

In 1952, 32 percent of all federal revenue came from the corporate income tax. Over the ensuing decades, this percentage has steadily declined. By the 1960s, corporate tax revenue averaged about 21 percent of all federal revenues. By the 1970s, it dropped to 15 percent and by the 1980s it was less than 10 percent.[13] By 2022, the corporate income tax accounted for a mere 9 percent of the revenue pie, with income taxes from individuals comprising 54 percent, and Social Security payroll taxes accounting for 30 percent.[14]

Unbelievably, the 2017 Trump tax cuts reduced corporate taxes even further. Post-2017, the largest profitable U.S. corporations saw their effective tax rates fall from an average of 22 percent to 12.8 percent. According to a May 2024 study by the Institute on Tax and Economic Policy, the 296 most profitable U.S. corporations paid $240 billion *less* in taxes between 2018 and 2021 than they did before the Trump tax cuts. While profits at the largest corporations soared by 44 percent in this period, their federal tax bills plummeted 16 percent. During these same years, the number of large profitable corporations paying less than effective rates of 10 percent increased from 56 to 95—including well-known megabrands such as Disney, Meta, Verizon, and Walmart.[15] Many of these companies used their tax cuts to buy back their stock rather than create jobs.[16]

Slashing taxes for the very richest American corporations is not only unfair—it's undemocratic. It shunts a greater share of tax obligations onto the 99 percent of Americans who are ordinary workers and middle-class professionals. It impoverishes the public purse, leaving our schools shabbier, our social spending on health care and housing far below that of other industrialized nations, and our roads and bridges in a state of increasing disrepair and danger.

Shift: Federal to State and Local Tax

Another feature of rising inequality over the past fifty years has been a shift in tax obligations from the federal government to states and localities. Sometimes called "devolution," the idea is to shift responsibility for services such as affordable housing, college access, community development, mental health, and so on to local and state governments. In many cases, this shift is accompanied by a reduction in support coming from the federal government and increased pressure on states and localities to finance those services.

This shift has happened stealthily over decades and has understandably created resentment about increasing local and state tax bills. But the average person doesn't know who is responsible for their rising property taxes or sales taxes. Allow me to connect the dots: *your local and state tax bills and fees have gone up over the last few decades because the billionaires are paying less in federal taxes.* Taxes that used to be paid by the wealthy at the federal level—producing the revenue that once subsidized local services—are now being paid by average Joes and Janes like you.

Localities that are starved of state and federal funds increasingly pay their bills by levying additional fees on residents for basic services or law enforcement. Thousands of cities across the United States routinely raise revenue for public services by imposing burdensome criminal justice fees and fines on defendants. These include fees for indigent defense services and police, jail, and court operations. To raise revenue, police departments aggressively issue tickets for the smallest of infractions in poor or Black neighborhoods, where residents have less political power to complain. This is the most regressive and racially discriminatory form of taxation, imposed on those with the least capacity to pay.[17] In Ferguson, Missouri, a majority Black city of roughly 21,000 people, police filed 11,400 cases for traffic infractions in 2013, the year before one of its officers killed teenager Michael Brown, a routine oppression that the Justice Department found helped to fuel the Black Lives Matter uprisings that followed.[18]

In another radical shift, the cost of higher education has been shifted from state and federal governments to tuition-paying families.[19] If you attended a public college or university after 2000, you may not realize that the federal and state governments provided significantly more support to higher education to students a generation before you. In California, the state university system was once the crown jewel of the nation's higher education system, and students attended essentially for free. This started to shift after several decades of state-level California tax cuts, including Prop 13 and Prop 77. In 2003, California repealed its state inheritance tax, losing $18 billion in revenue between 2003 and 2016. During this period, average in-state tuition and fees for public colleges rose nearly 70 percent after accounting for inflation. During the same period, student debt rose 17 percent along with the share of tuition paid by families. Meanwhile, the federal contribution to state higher education has shrunk.

Let's pause to emphasize how powerful and largely invisible this tax shift has been. Tax cuts at the federal level by and large have not reduced taxes for working people. And when you shift from levying progressive taxes from high incomes and inheritances at the federal level to comparatively regressive taxes at the state and local levels, you're effectively raising taxes on working and middle-class taxpayers. ("Progressive" in this context means the richer you are, the higher percentage of taxes you pay.) The federal government still has a somewhat progressive income tax rate structure, and modest taxes on inherited wealth, albeit increasingly ineffectual. Meanwhile, states have significantly more regressive tax systems, where lower-income people pay a higher percentage of their income than do wealthy taxpayers.

Revenue at the state and local levels is more dependent on sales, property, and flat excise taxes that fall on every resident equally, whether you're rich or poor. These are the regressive taxes paid by lower-income households, which are less able to afford them. Some states, such as Tennessee and South Dakota, levy sales taxes on groceries but resist having an income tax that would tax residents in proportion to their income.[20]

According to the National Conference of State Legislatures, "Those with lower incomes typically spend about three-quarters of their earnings on items that are subject to sales tax, whereas top earners spend about a sixth of their income on taxed items."[21] Across all states, the average percentage of income that low-income taxpayers shell out in state and local taxes is 60 percent higher than the percentage paid by the top 1 percent of households. The lowest-income 20 percent of households pay 11.4 percent of their income in state and local taxes; the middle 20 percent pay 10.5 percent; and the richest 1 percent pay a mere 7.2 percent.[22]

But this mix of regressive revenue sources varies widely by state. The Institute on Taxation and Economic Policy does a

Florida Taxes

2024 state and local taxes as a share of family income, shown at 2023 income levels

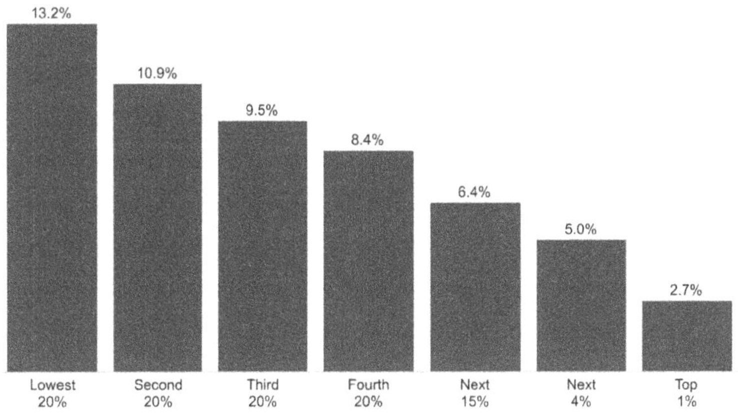

Source: Institute on Taxation and Economic Policy, *Who Pays?* (7th Edition), 2024.

periodic state-by-state report titled *Who Pays?* The state of Florida, for example, has one of the most regressive state tax systems in the country. The lowest-income fifth pays 13.2 percent of their income in Florida taxes, while the middle fifth pays 9.5 percent. Meanwhile, the richest 1 percent of Floridians pay only 2.7 percent of their incomes in Florida taxes, making it a favored tax haven of golf-playing billionaires.

Federal government support for states and localities had a brief revival during the COVID-19 pandemic, as emergency federal funds were appropriated through the CARES Act (Coronavirus Preparedness and Response Supplemental Appropriations) to help states and individuals weather the disaster, as businesses closed en masse. By 2022, some states were flush with cash and decided to cut taxes. Again, because the wealthy have more political clout, some states cut taxes that mostly affected the wealthy and corporations, not working people. What happens when you reduce income taxes while retaining or hiking sales taxes? Lower-income wage earners pay more. Billionaires benefit when states shift taxes off income and onto sales taxes or other more regressive fees.

In summary, tax reforms over the past several decades have aggressively moved responsibility off billionaires and the profitable corporations they own and onto working and middle-class wage earners. The math is simple: their tax bill goes down and yours goes up. Meanwhile, the popular narrative propagated by billionaires and anti-tax conservatives is that the Fortune 400 are doing so well solely because they are brilliant entrepreneurs, richly deserving of all that they have amassed.

HIDDEN WEALTH: TAX HAVEN USA

Our understanding of the inequality crisis is based on the income and wealth *that we know about*—that is, money that can be documented, measured, and sometimes taxed. But what about the vast amounts of wealth owned by the billionaire class that have been deliberately moved to the shadows, vanishing from the ledger?

Billionaires routinely pay millions to hide trillions. They do this by hiring an armada of tax attorneys, wealth managers, accountants, and family office staffers.[23]

As we discussed in chapter 1, most billionaires have their own family offices, which manage the assets of the global super-wealthy, all with the primary mission of wealth preservation over multiple generations. There are an estimated ten thousand family offices globally, serving as financial butlers to the billionaire class.[24] The three goals of the wealth defense enablers are to make the wealth pile bigger, minimize taxes, and maximize dynastic succession, the flow of wealth down the family bloodline. They work to create a two-tier tax system—one set of rules for the billionaires, another for everyone else.

These wealth defenders have a robust toolbox of dynasty trusts, anonymous companies, shell corporations, and offshore tax havens to do their work. They design "tax minimization" strategies for their wealthy clients and view tax payments as a failure.

Trillions of dollars are now vanishing into a hidden-wealth archipelago. Researchers estimate that some 10 to 12 percent of the world's wealth—trillions of dollars—is now hidden

THE POOR PAY TAXES...
THE RICH PAY ACCOUNTANTS
Lindsay

through a combination of tax-haven secrecy jurisdictions, shell companies, opaque trusts, and other mechanisms. The exact amount of hidden wealth is difficult to measure because . . . well, it is hidden! The Tax Justice Network estimates that between $24 trillion and $36 trillion is sequestered globally.[25]

Today's billionaires are increasingly stateless, detaching their money from nation-states and conventional representations of ownership to hide and preserve it. They obtain multiple passports from different countries and pit nations and jurisdictions against one another in a competition as to who will tax them least. This is a global tax regime best described as something between "catch me if you can" and "whack-a-mole."

THE RISE OF DYNASTIC WEALTH

If current trends of concentration continue, we will witness the rise of hereditary aristocracy of wealth and power similar to the monarchies of old, wherein the children of today's billionaires dominate our future economy, politics, culture, and philanthropy. If you think we've already arrived at that point, just wait another decade.

Inherited wealth—that is, "dynasties"—is generally focused on rigging the rules to protect and grow that wealth. There is sometimes an "incumbency protection" attitude among the billionaire class and their enablers, effectively pulling up the ladder and blocking opportunities for everyone else to become prosperous. Inherited wealth dynasties are incompatible with vibrant market economies and social mobility and also reinforce existing caste and racial economic divides.

"I MADE MONEY THE OLD FASHIONED WAY.
I INHERITED IT."

Unlike countries like England, France, and Spain, the United States doesn't have a tradition of aristocratic wealth dynasties lording over the populace. The American Revolution was fought to break free from England's aristocratic model of governance. Historically, great fortunes in this country have often diminished over multiple generations as money is spent, passed down to heirs, given to charity, and paid in taxes. Only when families aggressively intervene to arrest this cycle does wealth continue to expand over multiple generations, even as the number of heirs increases. Unfortunately, that's what's happening today.

In the thirty years after World War II, between 1945 and 1975, the rules of the economy focused on expanding opportunity and growing a white middle class. High incomes and inherited wealth were taxed at steeply progressive rates, to the benefit of the larger (white) populace. Under Republican president Dwight Eisenhower, the top income tax rate was a whopping 91 percent on very high incomes, and inheritances were subject to steep estate taxes.

Revenue from this progressive tax system was invested in government programs such as low-interest loans for first-time homebuyers, the GI bill and debt-free college, and infrastructure projects that benefited the wider public, not just the wealthy few.

These decades turn out to have been the golden age of relative U.S. equality. Since the late 1970s, we've reversed course, cutting taxes on the wealthy and sacrificing public investments in education, housing, and public services that benefit the non-wealthy. Our roads, bridges, and public infrastructure have a distinct last-century quality to them, something that becomes immediately apparent to those who have traveled to Europe or other industrialized countries, where their roads and public transportation systems gleam in comparison. In the face of weakened tax laws and aggressive hiding of wealth, the untaxed revenue of billionaires is going to their children and family members, instead.

Here's how bad it has become: In the early 1980s, *Forbes* magazine started publishing its infamous list of the four hundred wealthiest individuals in the United States. In 1983, there were only fifteen billionaires on the list, and the total combined net worth of the richest four hundred people was $118 billion.[26] Today, Elon Musk alone is worth over $400 billion.[27]

The country's three wealthiest families are the Waltons of Walmart, the Mars of the Mars candy empire, and the Koch family, heirs to energy conglomerate Koch Industries, one of the country's largest privately held companies. (David Koch died in August 2019, passing his wealth to his wife, Julia.) These three family enterprises, built by the grandparents and parents of today's heirs and heiresses, now possess more than $600 billion combined. Since 1983, these three families have seen their wealth increase more than 3,500 percent, adjusted for inflation. Over the same period, the median household wealth in the United States increased a mere 3 percent.[28]

THE WEAKENING OF THE ESTATE TAX

For a century, U.S. society had a strong mechanism to discourage dynastic wealth accumulation: the federal estate tax. In 1906, President Theodore Roosevelt said, "The man of great wealth owes a particular obligation to the State because he derives special advantages from the mere existence of government. It is only under the shelter of the civil magistrate that the owner of valuable property can sleep a single night in security."

Roosevelt was a champion of a federal estate tax, advocating for a "graduated inheritance tax on big fortunes, properly safeguarded against evasion and increasing rapidly in amount with the size of the estate." In 1916, partly in response to the excesses of Gilded Age capitalists, Congress passed a federal estate tax to put a brake on concentrations of wealth and power.[29]

Starting in 1997, anti-tax movements funded by dynastically wealthy families such as the Mars clan, the Gallos (of Gallo Winery), and the Waltons bankrolled an effort to repeal the estate tax. They didn't go out and say, "Save America's billionaires." Instead, they financed stealth campaigns to purposely confuse Americans as to *who* primarily paid the estate tax, arguing that it would be a death knell for small family farms and closely held, modest family businesses.

The Mars family offers a case study in estate tax avoidance over three generations. Estate tax attorney Bob Lord observes that the original fortune established by Forrest Mars Sr. passed upon his death to his three children in 1999 in its entirety, completely undiminished by taxes. And in 2017, the next generation received inheritances of $25 billion, equal to the parent's wealth. Lord writes that if Forrest Jr.'s "fortune had been subject to a significant estate tax after he passed on, the collective wealth of his four daughters in 2017 would be substantially less than that $25 billion."[30]

While the federal estate tax was not completely abolished in 2005, lawmakers have repeatedly doubled and tripled the exempted amount and failed to close loopholes that effectively gut the tax, culminating in the 2017 Trump tax cuts. As a result, only a minuscule percentage of very wealthy households pay the tax.

Billionaires have found loopholes for avoiding the tax, making it even more porous and toothless. ProPublica found that half of the country's wealthiest one hundred billionaires deploy a special trust called a grantor retained annuity trust (GRAT), which they have used to avoid some $100 billion in taxes over a thirteen-year period. The trust-loving, tax-dodging billionaires included Blackstone founder Stephen Schwarzman, cosmetic heir Leonard Lauder, media magnate Michael Bloomberg, the Koch brothers, and widow of Apple founder Steve Jobs.[31]

The late casino magnate Sheldon Adelson was number nineteen on the billionaires list when he died in 2021, with an estate worth $29.8 billion. Adelson set up a GRAT to pass on $7.9 billion in gifts to his children between 2010 and 2013, while avoiding $2.8 billion in gift and estate taxes.[32] While alive, Adelson broke spending records during the 2018 and 2020 national elections, with more than $100 million in campaign donations. In 2024, his widow, Miriam Adelson, was one of the three biggest donors to the Trump presidential campaign.[33]

The narrative of meritocracy becomes awfully attenuated within the dynastic redoubts of Billionaireville. It is a challenge to pretend your wealth is deserved when your main accomplishment in life was the fortuity of being born to wealthy parents or grandparents.

The justification for their inborn advantage must tap into other narratives than meritocracy. Among these dynastic wealthy, one hears supremacist talk of virtuous families with "good genes," more energy, and values of thrift, hard work, and other forms of inherent superiority. As Naomi Klein observes, "Only ideas like these can help justify a passion to avoid taxes on a pile of wealth that has been passed through four generations. You must believe there is something inherently superior about your family."[34]

Unrigging the tax code is a straightforward—if not a politically simple—endeavor. There are several commonsense fixes that would move us in the right direction, which I discuss in greater detail in chapter 12.

CHAPTER 6

BILLIONAIRES ARE WRECKING THE HOUSING MARKET

THE CONCENTRATION OF BILLIONAIRE WEALTH has harmed the physical security of millions of people in profound ways, through disruption of the housing market. Most U.S. communities are today facing an acute housing shortage, manifested in the growing numbers of unsheltered people, fierce competition for rental housing, and homeownership that increasingly lies out of reach for the average young family. You may well be experiencing one of these housing impacts yourself:

- You are unsheltered, doubled up in crowded housing, in a shelter or motel, or unable to quit a bad living situation or to live independently of your parents.
- You pay more than 50 percent of your monthly income on housing.
- You commute a long distance from work or school to find decent affordable housing.
- You aspire to own your own home, but this is out of reach due to the gap between your wages and

the salary required to be approved for a mortgage; or you saved money, have a stable income, and have been pre-approved for a mortgage, but you are unable to compete against affluent or investor buyers making cash offers that waive inspections.

* To buy your own home, you signed on to what you realize now is a scam—a rent-to-buy or contract-for-deed mortgage where you have all the responsibilities of a homeowner with none of the financial benefits. If you miss a payment, you lose everything you put into the house.

* You own a mobile home in a park, but you feel vulnerable because an investor could buy the park and jack up pad fees.

The data confirms that these scenarios are no longer the exception but increasingly the norm. On a single night in 2023, more than 650,000 people in the United States experienced homelessness, a 12 percent increase over the previous year.[1] A 2024 report found the number had increased to 770,000, a jump of 18 percent.[2] In 2022, half of all tenants in rental housing were "cost burdened," defined as paying more than 30 percent of their income for shelter, with a quarter considered "severely cost burdened" because they pay half their income for shelter.[3] And for prospective homebuyers, the gap between people's income and the cost of a home has widened. At the national level, the median sale price for a single-family home was almost six times higher than the median household income, up from a ratio of 4 to 1 as recently as 2019.[4]

Millions of households are in situations like this, living with the stress of housing insecurity or defeated dreams. Whether you experience your housing challenge as a personal failure, the result of a bad landlord, or a challenging market, the truth is that we are all caught up in a housing system that is horribly out of kilter—skewed because of billionaire disruption. A tiny sliver of wealthy individuals—in particular, their pools of investment cash—are supercharging gentrification, homelessness, unaffordable rental housing, and out-of-reach homeownership.

BILLIONAIRE DISRUPTION AND THE HOUSING CRISIS

Housing is both a basic human need and a commodity. It can be a wealth-building asset for low- and middle-income households—*and* a source of massive wealth extraction for billionaire investors.

What's happening in the housing market is a case study of how the wealth pump operates in a cycle of extraction, wealth defense, political capture, and hyper-extraction. As huge amounts of wealth have concentrated in the hands of a small group over the past four decades, real estate investors have ridden roughshod over the *decent and affordable housing for everyone* market, siphoning trillions from working families in the bottom 90 percent to absentee owners, private developers, and billionaire investors.

Concentrated wealth is disrupting the housing market in several direct and indirect ways:

* Inflaming traditional gentrification and displacement

* Accelerating multiple property acquisitions by wealthy buyers, thus reducing supply

* Driving the conversion of rental properties to short-term rentals, like Airbnb

* Increasing corporate ownership of rental housing, including single-family homes and mobile home parks

* Allowing global billionaires to park assets in U.S. real estate, driving up prices and reducing supply

In the early phase of housing wealth extraction, we find the owner of multifamily housing, earning rents. As a landlord's income increases, she acquires more property, charges more rents, and attracts more investment capital, or as they say in the business, OPM—"other people's money." At a certain stage, large property owners may use their wealth and influence to fend off regulation and ensure that lawmakers heed their interests.

Supercharged Gentrification

When wealthy people enter a lower-income neighborhood, they generally bid up the cost of land and housing, over time displacing lower-income residents, who are often renters. In the United States, the victims of gentrification are disproportionately people of color, who are forced to relocate to other communities. This is no longer just a problem within inner cities; increasingly in middle-income suburban communities, affluent buyers are tearing down smaller, older homes and building large houses on those lots, in the process reducing the supply of starter homes and driving up real estate prices in those places. These age-old dynamics of gentrification have been compounded by growing inequality at both ends of the spectrum—by the excessive wealth of today's rich people and by increasing economic precarity among the non-wealthy. This is leading not only to gentrification but also to a hyper-polarization of some cities and communities. In many cities, middle-class housing options have been hollowed out, leaving neglected public and private rental housing standing in the shadows of gleaming residential luxury towers. The billionaires are increasingly displacing the millionaires, and the millionaires are crowding out everyone else.

Multiple Property Acquisitions by the Wealthy

Extremely wealthy investors are purchasing property in multiple markets for their own luxury use but also as stable investments. It's not unusual for billionaire households to have five or more homes in different locales and cities, and sadly, many that sit vacant for most of the year. U.S. cities like New York, Los Angeles, Miami, San Francisco, Chicago, Washington, DC, Boston, and Dallas, among others, bear a heavy footprint of "occasional resident" billionaires.

Wealthy investors will often purchase condos in a luxury rental tower with no intention to occupy them, but purely as appreciating assets. Neither do they have any need to earn rent on such properties, which therefore sit vacant. "They are homes, but they are also investment vehicles for the global super-rich," writes Katherine Clarke in her book about New York City's luxury real estate boom, *Billionaires' Row: Tycoons, High Rollers, and the Epic Race to Build the World's Most Exclusive Skyscrapers.* "Some of the owners have never set foot in their own apartments, viewing them instead as one might a stock or bond or an artwork from a great master—a vessel in which to store wealth."[5]

Growing Investments in Short-Term Rentals

In certain markets, the expansion of short-term rentals like Airbnb and their smaller competitors like Vrbo are shrinking the number of apartments available on the market for full-time occupancy. Research shows a growing number of communities, especially in heavily touristed areas, are suffering from the "Airbnb effect," as landlords convert their long-term rentals to short-term occupancies for the higher return they offer.[6]

The problem is not so much a small owner or landlord with an additional apartment in their house. The most harmful impact is when whole houses and apartments are removed from the rental or sales market by owners with multiple properties, turning entire sections of communities into short-term rental market havens through concentrated ownership. One indication of the number of permanent conversions is that an estimated 25 percent of owners on sites like Airbnb operate fully two-thirds of its short-term rental listings.

Through private equity firms, billionaires are assembling pools of capital to invest in short-term and vacation rental companies, adding fuel to an already raging fire that is consuming affordable housing. For example, one Ohio real estate investing firm set up a $1.5 billion portfolio in 2021 for short-term rental acquisitions; as of May 2024, investors included the Blackstone Group, Harrison Street, and Davidson Kempner Capital Management, and three private equity firms with $1.14 trillion in assets under management. Short-term rental real estate investment trusts, through which investors bundle properties together to attract even more capital, will be the next emergent trend.

Jeff Bezos Wants to Be Your Landlord

Billionaire investment in the short-term rental market is part of a larger trend, as ownership of all rental properties shifts from local owners (so-called mom-and-pop landlords) to national corporate giants. Large private equity firms such as Blackstone and Apollo Capital are taking advantage of the tight housing market and declining homeownership rates to get into the business of single-family, long-term home rentals. Billionaire Jeff Bezos has recently invested in Arrived, a start-up real estate company buying up single-family rental properties.[7]

These billionaire investors see money to be made by snatching up single-family homes, often in foreclosure, and renting them to a large and growing segment of the population (including many higher-income households) that is locked out of homeownership. In 2022, these investor groups owned just 5 percent of the 14 million single-family home rentals nationally. But according to one forecast, investors are on track to hold 7.6 million homes—a full 40 percent of all single-family rentals—by 2030.[8]

The Country's Largest Private Equity Housing Barons

Equity Firm	Headquarters	Net Worth of Key People
1. Blackstone, Inc.	New York, NY	Stephen Schwarzman, $45.3 billion
2. Kohlberg Kravis Roberts (KKR)	New York, NY	Henry Kravis, $14.5 billion George Roberts (not pictured), $16.1 billion
3. TPG	Fort Worth, TX	David Bonderman, $6.9 billion Jim Coulter, $5.2 billion
4. The Carlyle Group	Washington, DC	David Rubenstein, $3.8 billion William Conway Jr. (not pictured), $4 billion Daniel D'Aniello (not pictured), $4.5 billion
5. Thoma Bravo	Chicago, IL	Carl Thoma (not pictured), $4.3 billion Orlando Bravo (not pictured), $9.8 billion

Sources: *Private Equity International* and *Forbes'* Real-Time Billionaires List. Photos from Getty Images.

In one section of North Minneapolis, private equity firms snatched up blocks and blocks of single-family rental housing and then neglected them. One corporate landlord, HavenBrook Homes, purchased 215 single-family homes scattered over several dozen residential blocks. A tenant organizer from United Renters was door knocking in the neighborhood and found that on every block there were four or five HavenBrook rental homes where residents didn't even know they had the same unresponsive landlord.[9]

Individual investors (not part of an investment group) are on the hunt, too. Investor purchases of single-family homes and multifamily rental properties have been on a steady rise, with 23 percent of residential sales in 2018, up from 16 percent in 2004.[10] Private investors acquired one in five homes sold in Greater Boston between 2004 and 2018, according to a report by the Metropolitan Area Planning Council.

The growing encroachment of wealthy investors in the housing market has not gone unnoticed by members of Congress. Senator Jeff Merkley (D-OR) told the *New York Times,* "You have created a situation where ordinary Americans aren't bidding against other families, they're bidding against the billionaires of America for these houses. And it's driving up rents and it's driving up home prices."[11]

Billionaires Are Even Buying Mobile Home Parks

Mobile homes—or "manufactured housing," as they are known in the industry—are an important source of affordable housing for an estimated 20 million households in the United States. A mobile home park is perhaps the last place you'd expect to find a billionaire, but similar to the single-family rental market, the billionaire private equity vultures have figured out that there is money to be extracted here, too. When they buy up parks, they squeeze residents for higher rents and fees, knowing that residents have few relocation options. Sociologist Esther Sullivan has documented these trends in her book, *Manufactured Insecurity: Mobile Home Parks and Americans' Tenuous Right to Place.* "The vulnerability of these residents is part of the business model. This is a captive class of tenant,"[12] she observes. Frank Rolfe, co-owner of a large corporate mobile home park company in the United States, once quipped that a manufactured home park "is like a Waffle House where the customers are chained to their booths."[13]

Since 2016, some of the nation's largest private investment firms have spent billions buying up mobile home parks from independent owners. The Carlyle Group, a private equity firm with an estimated $382 billion under management,[14] has been purchasing mobile home parks in Florida and California, concentrating on markets where technology companies have pushed up living costs and created more demand for mobile homes from people displaced by gentrification. Brookfield Asset Management, based in Toronto, acquired 135 mobile home parks in thirteen states. Other big players include Apollo Global Management, Blackstone Group, and Stockbridge Capital Group.[15]

In one instance, residents of an Iowa park learned that the land under their mobile homes was bought by RV Horizons, a firm owned by several foreign limited liability companies. The owners immediately hiked rents and began charging residents for water and trash removal, services that had been previously included in their rent.[16]

But there is some good news—mobile home park residents are organizing associations and buying their parks as cooperatives. And several states are passing laws to enable residents to have a first crack at buying their parks when they are put up for sale.[17]

Global Billionaires in the City

For the excessively wealthy at the top of the heap, investing in housing is a core strategy in wealth defense, a way to diversify and park a lot of assets. I described earlier the billionaire's challenge of diversifying their holdings across multiple "asset classes." Typical asset classes include shares in public corporations, Treasury bonds, venture capital, real estate, fine art, jewelry, gold, cryptocurrency, commodities, and everything else. Of these, real estate in the form of land, residential housing, commercial buildings, and recreational properties, spread over many geographical markets, is a particularly attractive way to diversify one's holdings. As Will Rogers astutely pointed out, "Buy land, they ain't making any more of it."

If you're a global billionaire, investing in U.S. and Canadian real estate is very attractive: North American real estate markets are stable, regulated, and geographically diverse and have historically held their value. And because the United States has become an attractive tax haven for global billionaires (more on this later), wealthy foreigners are increasingly looking to park their hidden trillions in U.S. real estate.

A significant portion of the estimated trillions in hidden wealth globally is literally being warehoused in the form of real property and luxury real estate. Across the world, skyscrapers and mansions are rising in international cities such as London, Hong Kong, New York City, and Panama, a form of safety-deposit box in the sky. Due to both international and domestic concentrations of wealth, many U.S. cities, especially those on the coasts, are experiencing a surge in luxury construction, with thousands of new high-end residential units in different stages of development. In Boston, thousands of new units of luxury housing are rising around the central city, with more than 5,000 such units in the permitting and construction pipeline, compared to less than half that number—only 2,100 units—of affordable housing planned.[18]

"One day, son, all these skyscrapers that we built for no reason and lie empty will be yours."

This trend supercharges existing gentrification dynamics, bidding up the cost of land and housing. Sadly, many of these units remain unoccupied.[19] In a painful irony, Los Angeles is experiencing a crisis of empty homes alongside an acute and growing tide of homelessness, with an estimated 36,000 unhoused families in the city. One report found more than 103,000 vacant units in Los Angeles, with more than 41,000 not even up for sale.[20] Tens of thousands of housing units are being withheld from the market by speculators and anonymous ownership entities (including trusts, LLCs, and shell corporations) that are simultaneously overproducing luxury housing, fueling residential displacement and homelessness, and increasing housing costs. Of the twenty-five luxury condominium buildings profiled in the report, 2,399 of 3,244 units, or 71 percent on average, are sitting vacant, because they are not anyone's primary residence—in effect "surplus" housing so expensive it can do nothing to ease the city's affordability crisis.

Many luxury buyers are using anonymous shell companies to mask the identity of the real owners, often because they are laundering money or avoiding publicity and public scrutiny. Secrecy is a growing value among the oligarch class, most of whom don't want the public to really know what they own, the location of their residences, and where their jets and yachts are parked. In 2014, 54 percent of real estate valued at more than $5 million was acquired in the name of anonymous shell companies.[21] Today, anonymous shell companies own 40 percent of the rental housing market, an estimated 18 million out of 48 million rental units nationwide, according to census data.[22]

A decade from now, the skylines, as well as the demographics, of many U.S. cities will be transformed by a handful of global billionaires—none of them residents of those cities.

Billionaires in the Countryside

A similar trend is apparent in rural areas, with large foreign shell companies based in Canada and China representing dynastic wealthy people snatching up and hoarding hundreds of thousands of acres.[23] The biggest owner of farmland in the United States is not Conagra or another agribusiness, but none other than Microsoft founder Bill Gates, who owns a staggering 260,000 acres, mostly in Montana. Gates's land acquisitions are overseen by Cascade Investment, his personal investment managers, as part of his "diversified portfolio."[24]

Gates may own a lot of farmland, but there are other billionaires who own millions of acres of timberland. The very largest U.S. landowner is Red Emmerson and his family, who own 2.4 million acres in California, Oregon, and Washington through their timber company, Sierra Pacific Industries. Other mega-landowners hail from oil and gas dynasties, like the Bass (285,000 acres) and Hughes (319,000 acres) families of Texas, who have diversified their holdings beyond "black gold" oil into land.[25]

The largest foreign landowner in the United States is the Irving family, from New Brunswick, Canada (owner of the Irving chain of gas stations), with 1.27 million acres of timberland in Maine, making them the largest private landowner in the state. The second-largest foreign landowner in the United States is Chinese billionaire Chen Tianqiao, a video game magnate who recently acquired 198,000 acres of timberland in Oregon.[26]

FIXING THE HOUSING PROBLEM

Local communities do not have to wait for the federal government to act. They can protect existing affordable housing and generate revenue for building new stock in several ways:

- Expand resident ownership with support for tenant-option-to-buy legislation for rental housing and mobile home parks, along with technical assistance and financing to expand resident ownership and control.

- Discourage mass wealth parking with rules requiring ownership transparency, so we know who is buying our neighborhoods (and so public bodies can regulate harmful behaviors and tax transactions to fund social housing). This could include passing ordinances prohibiting keeping units vacant for long periods of time.

* Raise revenue for permanently affordable housing and expand resident-owned housing and mobile home parks with transfer taxes on luxury real estate, with funds dedicated to social housing. This could include taxes on vacancies and empty homes.

* Rein in billionaire investor disruption with limitations on corporate ownership of housing and controls on short-term rentals to prevent contraction of the long-term rental market.

CHAPTER 7

BILLIONAIRES ARE SUPERCHARGING THE RACIAL ECONOMIC DIVIDE

BILLIONAIRES ARE FUELING A SYSTEM OF HEREDITARY wealth and power that reinforces and compounds existing racial economic disparities. These modern-day dynasties are benefiting from trillions of dollars of intergenerational wealth transfers among the super-wealthy, primarily in white families.

The present-day racial economic divide is, of course, a consequence of a long and multigenerational story of Indigenous land theft, chattel slavery, and centuries of discrimination in employment and housing. It is a legacy in which the past is present, manifested in gaping disparities between the wealth of white, Native, and Black families in particular.

Several decades of shared economic prosperity between 1945 and 1975 began to narrow economic disparities between the races. But as the rules of the economic system have skewed toward billionaires, historic racial wealth inequalities have been "supercharged."

On the sixtieth anniversary of the 1963 March on Washington, where the Reverend Martin Luther King Jr. delivered his "I Have a Dream" speech, the Institute for Policy Studies, the organization for which I work, published a study on the economic progress of Black Americans. It found that Black Americans have made substantial socioeconomic advances since the 1960s, across several measures:[1]

* **Poverty.** In 1963 Black Americans had a poverty rate of 51 percent, compared to 15 percent for white Americans. By 2021, poverty rates had declined, with white poverty at 8 percent and Black poverty at 20 percent. Though this is a substantial decline, it still means almost one in five Black Americans continue to live in poverty, compared to one in twelve white Americans.

* **Educational Attainment.** The rate of Black high school attainment has increased sharply over the last six decades, rising from 24.8 percent in 1962 to 90.1 percent in 2022. The white-Black college attainment gap has also narrowed over sixty years but remains substantial. In 1962, white adults were 2.4 times more likely to complete college than Black adults; today, they are 1.7 times as likely to have a college degree.

* **Employment.** Unemployment has been historically low for Black Americans over the last decade. Between 1974 and 1994, Black unemployment consistently remained in the double digits, with rates twice as high as those for white Americans. Between 1994 and 2017, Black unemployment rates dropped, varying between 7 percent and 10 percent, occasion-

ally spiking to nearly 17 percent during recessions. However, since 2018, Black unemployment has reached record lows of 5 percent and 6 percent, except during the eighteen-month recession caused by the COVID-19 pandemic.

* **Income and Wealth: Slow Progress.** While the gains in poverty, education, and employment are positive examples of Black economic progress, most socio-economic markers are changing so slowly that it would take centuries to reach something even close to parity. For example, for every dollar of white family income in 1967, African American households earned just 58 cents. But decades later, in 2021, African American households earned just a few pennies more—62 cents for every white household's dollar. At this slow rate, it would take Black households 513 years to reach income parity with white households. Median household income for Black Americans has grown just 0.36 percent since the turn of the century, and after adjusting for inflation, it is still lower than the median income of white families in 1963.

* **Homeownership.** Since homeownership is often the first step in establishing individual wealth, it is worth tracking progress in narrowing the homeownership gap. Black homeownership increased from 38.2 percent in 1960 to 44.3 percent in 2022, an increase of 6 percentage points. White homeownership has increased from 64.9 percent in 1960 to

> 73.1 percent in 2022, a 10 percent increase. Over the past six decades, however, the white-Black homeownership divide has held steady, slightly worsening from a gap of 26.7 percent to 27.8 percent. Meanwhile, in recent years, Latino and Asian American families both experienced their highest average homeownership rates. The Latino homeownership rate rose to 51.1 percent and Asian American homeownership rose to 63.2 percent, but both still lag the 73.3 percent homeownership rate of white families.[2]

The Survey of Consumer Finances, sponsored by the Federal Reserve and released every three years, is a rich trove of data on household wealth. The survey was last published in 2022, and it revealed that in that year the average wealth gap between white families and Black and Latino families reached a new high, topping $1 million in household wealth. The surveys found that the average wealth of Latino families in 2022 was $227,000, while the average Black family held wealth of $211,000. The wealth of white families eclipsed both groups by more than $1 million more—an average of $1.3 million.[3]

Averages, however, include the wealth of white billionaires, of which there are many more than billionaires of color. Upper Richistan and Billionaireville are among the most racially segregated neighborhoods in the United States. Looking at *median* wealth tells a different story, one less distorted by billionaire assets. Even so, racial wealth disparities are striking. In 2022, the median Black family had $44,000 in wealth while the median Latino family had $62,000. The median white family, on the other hand, possessed wealth of $284,000. The difference between median wealth and average wealth is important, but both tell necessary stories about money and race. Median wealth statistics tell us more about the experiences of the typical family, while wealth data that reports averages reveals a chasm of wealth inequality—and who sits at the top.

Wealth statistics require scrutiny to grasp the full picture. For example, the 2022 survey found that Asian Americans had the highest average family wealth of any group at $1.8 million.[4] But other research has shown that household finances vary greatly *between* segments of Asian Americans, with those in the ninetieth percentile earning nearly eleven times as much as those in the bottom 10 percent.[5]

A critical indicator of well-being is how many households have zero or negative wealth, with no financial reserves to fall back upon. More than 15 percent of the households in the U.S. population have net wealth less than or equal to zero, while 14 percent have strictly negative wealth.[6] But looking through the racial lens, 25 percent of Black households have zero or negative wealth compared to 8 percent of white households.[7]

SUPERCHARGING RACIAL ECONOMIC INEQUALITY

It is important to situate these statistics about the racial economic divide in the context of a political economy dominated by billionaires. The acceleration of wealth inequality within all racial groups has steadily widened as much of the wage and wealth gains in the past twenty years have flowed upward not just to the top 1 percent of households but to the top 0.1 percent of households and the billionaire class.

These regressive economic trends have only supercharged historic racial wealth disparities. In the thirty years after the Second World War, between 1947 and 1977, overall income and wealth inequality declined. During these decades, the disparity between Black and white wages also began to narrow. Homeownership and median wealth gaps also shrank. Had the postwar trajectory of rising wages and expanding middle-class standards of living continued, it is likely that racial disparities would have also declined. Instead, those positive trends slowed and then reversed beginning in the 1980s for the reasons identified in earlier chapters: changes in the rules of the economy (tax policy, wage policy, public investments) that benefited asset owners at the expense of wage earners.

Because of cuts to the estate tax and myriad tax avoidance strategies, hereditary wealth and power are increasing. According to UBS, the Swiss bank favored by the superrich, the current generation of billionaires collect more wealth from inheritances than work.[8] And the 1,023 global billionaires who are over seventy are likely to transfer $5.2 trillion to their heirs over the coming decades. These dynastic fortune holders have vested interests in opposing inheritance taxes and lobbying against investments that would foster opportunity and mobility for the bottom 99.9 percent.

In short, large intergenerational wealth transfers among the superrich reinforce and exacerbate racial divisions in income, wealth, and opportunity by preventing the distribution of some of that wealth to others in society through taxation and government investment in early childhood education, health care, debt-free higher education, jobs, and skills training—all things that foster upward mobility for the rest of society.

FIXES

There are a wide range of specific solutions that would narrow the racial economic divide. These include the following:

* A push for full employment, including a guaranteed job of last resort (like the Works Progress Administration provided during times of recession)
* A massive federal homeownership program, with low-interest mortgages and meaningful down payment assistance loans and grants
* A commitment to individual asset building, through programs like "baby bonds" that give each newborn a nest egg that can be tapped into in young adulthood
* Targeted reparations and universal health care to close multigeneration disparities and boost the next generation

Some of these remedies are universal and would lift people of all races, including whites left behind in these last four decades of inequality. But to repair the four centuries of this breach, it's becoming increasingly clear that reparations and repair for Native American dispossession and Black slavery and its legacy—including Jim Crow—must be part of the equation.

Facing what activist Randall Robinson calls "the debt" to people of African descent and Native Americans means confronting the reality that lighter skin color conferred, and continues to confer, economic advantage. To pretend otherwise is to live a destructive lie, perpetuating a perverted myth of meritocracy that holds back our entire society.

To that end, political and logistical challenges of reparations must be worked out. But one thing is clear: investments in repair and reparations should be paid for by a steeply graduated tax on billionaire wealth, in particular by taxing inheritances at a higher rate.

Why? One of the most common objections to reparations is that it unfairly puts the burden on the present generation of white people to pay for the "sins of their parents." But if that is so, what is the argument for allowing individuals to inherit vast amounts of dynastic wealth earned by their parents or grandparents or ancestors stretching back generations? These individuals can hardly be said to have "earned" that wealth. Yet that kind of dynastic wealth was often accumulated in the first place through stolen land, free labor, and suppressed wages extracted from people of color. Given this history, taxation on inherited wealth should perhaps be the first place we look to finance programs to increase homeownership, higher education, and other wealth-boosting strategies for historically excluded groups.

CHAPTER 8

BILLIONAIRES ARE BAD FOR YOUR HEALTH

THE GROWTH IN THE NUMBER OF BILLIONAIRES IN THE United States is bad for your health.

A variety of fascinating research over the last two decades has found that the more unequal a society, the worse its health outcomes are, regardless of your economic status.[1] And the more a society grows its class of billionaire investors, the more the health care system becomes a target of wealth extraction through for-profit hospitals, Big Pharma, and the private insurance system that fleece and fail patients. In other words, we are growing a class of billionaires whose fortunes have been plundered from a for-profit health system that sacrifices the well-being of ordinary people for the benefit of shareholders, overpaid CEOs, and private equity firms.

HEALTH VERSUS OUR HEALTH CARE SYSTEM

There is an important distinction to be made between "health" and the American health care system. In the United States, we like to pride ourselves in our high-tech health care sector, with our gleaming diagnostic machines, miracle drugs, and heroic surgical interventions to prolong life. But advanced medical tools are distinct from our actual physical and mental health.

In the United States, we spend a higher percentage of our income on the health care system than other industrialized countries, yet we have some of the worst health indicators of that group of nations. In 2022, the United States spent a collective $4.4 trillion on health care, roughly $13,493 per person per year. This represents 17.3 percent of the country's GDP or a sixth of the total U.S. economy.[2] This is almost twice the average per capita expenditure of other OECD countries and $4,500 a year more than the next highest-spending countries of Switzerland and Germany.[3] But does this buy us health?

Most health status indices consider multiple measures, including life expectancy, avoidable mortality (premature deaths that could have been prevented or treated), diabetes prevalence (as an indicator of chronic disease), and self-rated health as a holistic measure of mental and physical health. The United States rates in the middle or the bottom of the pack on most of these indicators. Average life expectancy in the United States is 76.4 years, behind every major OECD country except Hungary. The United States is among the top four countries with adults living with diabetes, including Mexico, Chile, and Turkey. U.S. infant mortality is the second highest of seventeen top OECD countries, after Costa Rica.[4]

In short, our for-profit health system delivers little in the way of good health. As health scholar Stephen Bezruchka writes, "When it comes to our health, we are far from the best. We have higher infant mortality, higher child and maternal mortality, live shorter lives, and suffer more chronic illness."[5] Furthermore, the poorer you are, the fewer benefits the medical system offers.[6] If the United States has such a great health system, Bezruchka asks, why don't we have the healthiest people, as measured by indicators like longevity? Almost all the longest-living people on the planet live outside the United States, with many in Japan and equitable European societies. Even Japanese men who smoke have significantly better health outcomes than all U.S. men. Billionaire involvement in our health care system has only worsened the picture.

BILLIONAIRE EXTRACTION FROM THE U.S. HEALTH CARE SYSTEM

The size of the U.S. health care system makes it a prime target for wealth extraction by billionaire investors. A century ago, most of our hospitals were founded by religious orders and civic leaders, and most of them were nonprofits with a focus centered on patient health.[7] Today, a growing percentage of the health care system is run by billionaire financiers and for-profit corporations.

As we have seen in the housing chapter, billionaire private equity funds have moved into every sector of the economy, hunting for businesses to squeeze and plunder. But applying private equity's cost-cutting, asset-selling, price-gouging techniques to health care has deadly consequences because it puts patients and practitioners at risk. The private equity business model "puts pressure on doctors to increase volumes of patients seen per day," write Eileen Appelbaum and Rosemary Batt in their extensive research about private equity.[8] It incentivizes doctors to "overprescribe diagnostic tests or perform unnecessary procedures, or to save on costs by using shoddier but less costly supplies and devices."

In their book, *These Are the Plunderers: How Private Equity Runs—and Wrecks—America,* Gretchen Morgenson and Josh Rosner chronicle the methods that privateers deploy to strip-mine health care operations. The playbook includes increasing charges on patients and slashing personnel costs, often replacing higher-cost doctors with less costly clinicians, such as nurse practitioners and physician assistants. The plunderers sell off hospital real estate assets to subsidiaries they control, requiring them to then pay high rents for the buildings they previously owned. They create additional subsidiary corporations and require their hospitals to contract with them for services. A hospital might buy administrative or debt-collection services from a company affiliated with the private equity owners, rather than from the best or lowest-cost supplier.

Morgenson and Rosner observe that the private equity titans "target hospital emergency departments, typically the most profitable unit of a hospital, and acquire doctor's groups, especially in lucrative specialties such as dermatology, radiology, and anesthesiology."[9] In each of these transactions, the private equity owners extract fees, even if it means the original company must take on additional debt to pay them. These increased costs are paid by taxpayers through Medicaid and Medicare, or through private insurers and out-of-pocket fees.

At the onset of the COVID-19 pandemic in 2020, two of the wealthiest U.S. private equity firms, Blackstone and KKR, had secured contracts to run more than one-third of the nation's emergency rooms.[10] By 2021, 11 percent of nursing homes and 40 percent of emergency rooms were owned by private equity firms.[11]

This financialization and hyper-extraction have fueled hospital bankruptcies and closures. I witnessed this happen in my own Boston community when a private equity firm, Cerberus Capital, bought the Caritas Christi/Carney Hospital, owned by the Roman Catholic Archdiocese of Boston, in 2010. Cerberus rebranded their hospital holdings as Steward Health Care and quickly began to pillage my neighborhood hospital, selling land and buildings for $1.2 billion to a closely affiliated real estate investment trust called Medical Properties Trust. Steward Health Care then began to pay rent on real estate it previously owned. Steward took on additional debt to pay Cerberus an $800 million fee. Steward's founder and CEO, billionaire Ralph de la Torre, paid himself tens of millions in compensation, purchasing a yacht worth $40 million.[12] Meanwhile, medical services at Steward's Carney Hospital became so diminished that patients and staff referred to it as "Carnage Hospital."[13] A group of medical residents urged the graduate education accreditation agency to shut down Carney's faltering residency program.[14]

By May of 2024, Steward Health Care had declared bankruptcy, a development that is jeopardizing health care services at Carney and six other Massachusetts hospitals. Among its bankruptcy claims, Steward owes more than $7 billion to Medical Properties Trust, the entity that owns the real estate and land under its hospitals, along with $2 billion to other lenders and contractors they stiffed. Meanwhile, investors like Cerberus have taken their fees and run. As of this writing, Massachusetts state officials have proposed to take over the hospitals by eminent domain.[15] In this way, private equity is literally sucking community health systems dry, leaving residents without health providers and the government to clean up the wreckage.

As part of an investigation into Steward Health Care, U.S. senator Ed Markey commissioned a report that reviewed fifty-five studies of the impact of private equity on the health care industry. The study found that "across the outcome measures, [private equity] ownership was most consistently associated with increases in costs to patients or payers. Additionally, PE ownership was associated with mixed to harmful impacts on quality." These harms included 32 percent higher costs to patients and insurers, lower staff-to-patient ratios, and patients suffering 25 percent more hospital-acquired complications.[16]

When the billionaire vultures fixed their talons on the U.S health system as a new source of profit, they focused on bill collection and other techniques for squeezing medical payments out of customers. You probably have firsthand experience with a medical billing department. If you or a family member has experienced a medical emergency in the last decade, you are probably familiar with getting a bevy of unexpected bills from different vendors within the system: the ambulance, the emergency room, the MD group, the anesthesiologist, the radiologist, and so on. And you may have even shelled out an outlandish fee to park at the for-profit parking garage next to the hospital, probably owned by the same private equity company or a group of cronies that bought the hospital. All this is a symptom of aggressive profiteering within the health industry, such that the number one cause of bankruptcy in the United Sates today is medical debt.[17]

In the United States, administrative costs—largely driven by private insurers—comprise 35 percent of health care expenses, double the percentage in Canada. Yet 8 percent of the U.S. population has no health insurance coverage, and an estimated 43 percent are underinsured.[18]

BAN PRIVATE EQUITY FROM OWNING HEALTH CARE FACILITIES AND OTHER CRITICAL SERVICES

An outright ban on for-profit ownership of hospitals and critical care facilities could protect the health and welfare of the public and limit the wealth extraction. Journalist Bethany McLean argued that increased regulation of private equity won't likely curtail the worst behaviors. "The only real solution is to pass laws preventing private equity ownership of certain critical businesses. Extractive capitalism should flourish only where it can't kill people," wrote McLean in the *Washington Post.*

PUBLIC HEALTH AND THE EPIDEMIC OF INEQUALITY

Despite the massive costs of our health care system, the most important factors contributing to improved health and increased longevity of Americans over the past century are what epidemiologists call an improvement in "public health" measures. These include better hygiene, separating sewage from drinking water, and cultural shifts such as encouraging handwashing and covering mouths when coughing. In recent decades, the most important life-extending public health practices have been efforts to discourage smoking, increase motor vehicle safety, improve workplace conditions, promote exercise and diet to reduce heart disease, and reduce infectious disease through infection control and immunization.[19] Ralph Nader's work to promote seat belts and boost auto safety has done more to contribute to real health and longevity than many so-called miracle drugs.

On the negative end of the spectrum, today the biggest threat to our physical and mental health is the rise of economic inequality. Four decades of accelerating inequality have steadily dropped the U.S. standing on key health measures. I will discuss later in this chapter how this is happening. But the important lesson is that *the more an economy increases the wealth of billionaires, the greater the declines in health.*

Health experts such as epidemiologist Richard Wilkinson, researcher Kate Pickett, and physician Stephen Bezruchka have all documented the ways in which inequality correlates with negative health indicators. It is no surprise that poverty and deprivation correlate with poor health outcomes. But it is in the gap between extreme wealth and the rising precarity and poverty of everyone else where we find the largest drivers of poor health.

From a health perspective, extreme inequality correlates with high rates of crime and other societal dysfunction. "Bigger gaps between rich and poor are accompanied by high rates of homicide and imprisonment," write Wilkinson and Pickett, authors of the groundbreaking 2009 book, *The Spirit Level: Why Equality Is Better for Everyone*. "They also correspond to more infant mortality, obesity, drug abuse, and COVID-19 deaths, as well as higher rates of teenage pregnancy and lower levels of child well-being, social mobility and public trust."[20] They write, "Even affluent people would enjoy a better quality of life if they lived in a country with a more equal distribution of wealth, similar to a Scandinavian nation. They might see improvement in their mental health and have a reduced chance of becoming victims of violence; their children might do better at school and be less likely to take dangerous drugs."

Between 2014 and 2017, before the COVID-19 pandemic began, the United States saw a startling decline in life expectancy for the first time since 1933. One factor identified by Princeton researchers Angus Deaton and Anne Case is what they call "deaths of despair," including suicide, alcoholism, and drug overdoses.[21] These deaths are concentrated among the working class and the two-thirds of the U.S. population who don't have a four-year college degree. Deaton and Case note that these trends are driven by several decades of growing inequality, in particular stagnant wages, rising health care costs, and declining dignity at work, as many workers don't feel respected and valued for their day's labor.

In U.S. culture, we focus on narratives of individual merit and hard work as the drivers of success in life, while discounting the role of luck. "Those who succeed tend to feel that if you did not make it, that is your fault, which makes them smug and sometimes contemptuous," said Deaton in an interview. "The people left behind think the system is rigged against them, which is increasingly true, but there is also this horrible feeling that maybe it is their fault. The combination of these two things leads to a tremendous amount of resentment. Condescension and contempt on one side and resentment on the other is heady and dangerous."[22] This combination leads to a toxic brew of rage, distrust, and self-harm.

In their 2020 book, *The Inner Level,* Wilkinson and Pickett examine the impact of inequality on mental and psychological well-being. They write, "The reality is that inequality causes real suffering, regardless of how we choose to label such distress. Greater inequality heightens social threat and status anxiety, evoking feelings of shame which feed into our instincts for withdrawal, submission and subordination: when the social pyramid gets higher and steeper and status insecurity increases, there are widespread psychological costs."[23] Note that these harms touch the wealthy as well as the poor and everyone in between.

Extreme inequality was a significant risk factor for the United States as it entered the 2020 COVID-19 pandemic, a key factor that contributed to its abysmally high mortality rates as compared with other industrialized nations. These inequality factors included unequal access to doctors, poor people living in cramped quarters, large numbers of incarcerated people unable to socially distance, and higher mortality rates among Native Americans, Black individuals, and Latinos.[24] The fact that our health care system had been pillaged by billionaire private equity investors in the decade before the pandemic also undermined our readiness.

STRESS

Billionaire-dominated unequal societies feature high levels of stress, even for billionaires themselves. The stress emerges from competition for survival and status, or "rankism." Stress releases cortisol hormones that fuel inflammation, which wreaks havoc on our bodies when sustained over time. Just as racism and poverty have been shown to contribute to stress and early death among Black people (a phenomenon known as "racial weathering"[25]), the stress of what philosopher Alain de Botton calls "status anxiety" also contributes to poor health outcomes, even among the wealthy.[26] When junk-bond trader Michael Milken appeared on the *Forbes* 400 richest list, a friend congratulated him. Milken's deflated response was, "But I'm on the bottom." Worry over "pecking order" status is endemic to societies with gargantuan wealth gaps.[27]

In his memoir, *Superyacht Captain,* Brendan O'Shannassy recounts touring a billionaire superyacht owner around the picturesque harbor of Cala di Volpe in Sardinia in a skiff. The owner asked O'Shannassy to detail the features of each yacht they passed—the length, cost, ownership—something the veteran captain could easily do, like a sports fan rattling off statistics about his favorite team. As the harbor tour continued, the superyacht owner became increasingly agitated. "Take me back to my yacht, please," he finally barked. After a few minutes of silence he added, "There was a time when my yacht, 60 meters, was the most beautiful boat in the bay. How do I keep up with this new money?" O'Shannassy observes that even great wealth does not quell status anxiety. "Even with immense wealth he was comparing himself to his peers and feeling dissatisfied. This is biological and sociological." He concludes, "There is no upper limit to competitive restlessness."[28]

As the philosopher de Botton observes, in caste and aristocratic societies where one's station in life is defined at birth and largely fixed, there is less status anxiety. In a culture of meritocracy, where one's rank is believed to be a function of effort and ability, low status takes on a moral taint. The cruelest hoax, one increasingly embodied in the contemporary United States, is to *claim* to be a meritocratic society while effectively operating like a caste society, with limited mobility in fact. As de Botton writes, "To the injury of poverty, a meritocratic system now added the insult of shame."

EARLY CHILDHOOD HEALTH

Another contributing factor to U.S. poor health is a national failure to invest in the early stage of life. "Half of our health factors are determined by the age of two," said Stephen Bezruchka in an interview.[29] The first thousand days of life, including nine months in utero, are the most critical to lifelong health. Chronic diseases such as diabetes, kidney disease, and heart disease have origins early in life. Many can be traced to experiences of stress, trauma, and poverty across generations. "When you have a high gap between the billionaires and everyone else, money flows to the top and not to investments in early life," said Bezruchka. "This is why the U.S. has no paid maternity/paternity leave, no free childcare and pre-school." The brief institution of a refundable Child Tax Credit during the pandemic demonstrated the positive impact that alleviating poverty could have on childhood health and development. Researchers found "Child poverty, as measured by the Supplemental Poverty Measure (SPM), fell from 9.7 percent in 2020 to 5.2 percent in 2021 but returned to pre-pandemic levels (12.4 percent) in 2022 after the CTC [Child Tax Credit] expansion expired."[30]

TRUST

The trust and social cohesion predicate to a healthy society break down as inequality grows. As societies pull apart, the distance between economic and racial subgroups increases, leading to a breakdown in trust and solidarity—that is, the sense that we are "in this together." In an atomized and unequal society, it is rational to pursue individual security and ignore societal interconnection and well-being.

In public surveys, societies with more "social capital"—in other words, networks, relationships, civic organizations, and local participation—score as having higher levels of trust. In more equitable societies, Richard Wilkinson writes, "the individualism and values of the market are restrained by social morality. People are more likely to be involved in social and voluntary activities outside the home. These societies have more of what has been called 'social capital,' which lubricates the workings of the whole society and economy. There are fewer signs of anti-social aggressiveness and society appears more caring. In short, the social fabric is in better condition."[31]

Higher-trust societies weathered the COVID-19 pandemic in better shape. The abysmal U.S. performance during the crisis was greatly undermined by a breakdown in trust; think here about the heated arguments about masking and shutdown mandates that prevailed in many communities, and the general distrust and outright antipathy of many people toward the instructions of government health officials.

As you think about the stresses on our health care system, remember that the billionaires bear huge responsibility. The longer waits, the hurried doctors, and the unexpected bills coming from multiple medical offices—these are all symptoms of the ways that concentrated wealth and an appetite for greater "returns on investment" are jeopardizing your health and undermining our wider well-being.

CHAPTER 9

BILLIONAIRES ARE STEALING YOUR VOTE AND VOICE

BILLIONAIRES ARE ROBBING YOU OF YOUR VOICE AND VOTE in a democracy teetering on the edge of plutocracy. With their inordinate wealth and power, billionaires are hijacking our political system with their campaign contributions, paid lobbyists, communications firms, and dark money contributions.

Shawn Fain, president of the United Auto Workers, describes the new era of billionaire capture of American politics in blunt terms:

> We're in a vicious cycle where the billionaire and corporate class take more and more for themselves and rewrite the rules of the game to keep it that way. They use their insane wealth to buy off politicians and elections. The lap dogs of the billionaires then pass more laws that restrict unions and keep working-class people down. They consolidate the fruits of our labor into the hands of Wall Street and corporate America, and that cycle goes on and on. It is an embarrassment to our democracy when billionaires can openly buy elections. But it's also a devastating situation for the working class.[1]

Because of the high cost of political campaigns, wealthy donors effectively narrow the field of candidates—those who can attract their funding—and which issues are discussed. Once in office, these billionaire-funded candidates block popular reforms and advance a fat cat–sanctioned agenda.

It's a simple dynamic. As wealth concentrates in fewer hands, so does political power. As I discussed in early chapters, the billionaires are deploying this power to change the rules to enable them to accumulate further wealth and power (or block policies that might tax and regulate them). The cycle

"I own one plane, two yachts, four houses and five politicians."

continues in ever more constricting fashion, in what Ezra Klein has described as the "Doom Loop of Oligarchy."[2]

For example, a conservative plutocracy has endeavored successfully in recent decades to reshape the Supreme Court and to eliminate campaign finance limits, making it easier for billionaires to buy a political system beholden to the donor class.

CAPTURED CAMPAIGNS

The billionaire impact on our election system was on full display in the 2024 national elections, where presidential candidates Donald Trump and Kamala Harris both received donations from dozens of billionaires, among them Miriam Adelson, Michael Bloomberg, and Elon Musk. Indeed, Elon Musk financed entire get-out-the-vote canvassing operations on behalf of Donald Trump, late in the campaign. Musk became America's largest political donor in 2024, plowing $277 million into the Republican campaigns.[3]

One of the wealthiest billionaires from the first Gilded Age is still wielding power in our political system more than a century later. In 1869, banker and industrialist Thomas Mellon was one of the wealthiest people in the world, having founded a Pittsburgh bank serving industrialists like Andrew Carnegie and Henry Frick. Thomas Mellon's son, Andrew Mellon (1855–1937), used his family wealth to help elect Warren Harding as president in 1920 and thereafter served as secretary of the Treasury under Presidents Harding, Calvin Coolidge, and Herbert Hoover. Secretary Mellon particularly hated the inheritance tax—what we today call in the United

States "the estate tax"—which slows the concentration of dynastic wealth. As Treasury secretary, Andrew Mellon worked with great success to cut the top tax rate from 73 percent to 25 percent.[4] This is political capture at its finest—the fox literally appointed as guardian of the henhouse.

Four generations later, this dynastically wealthy family is still deploying its considerable influence. Timothy Mellon, great-grandson of Thomas Mellon, was one of the largest donors to the 2024 elections, having invested $20 million in Robert F. Kennedy Jr.'s campaign and $100 million for Donald Trump, in addition to $30 million each for super PACs for Republican House and Senate candidates. Mellon also gave $54 million to Texas governor Greg Abbott's border wall fund.

Mellon, a reclusive billionaire who lives on a ranch in Wyoming, is worth an estimated $1 billion. The Mellon clan is the thirty-fourth wealthiest U.S. family, with assets estimated by *Forbes* of $14.1 billion.[5] In addition to his love of inherited wealth and power, Timothy Mellon is a fierce opponent of social welfare. The fourth-generation heir "rages only against those handouts that go to those born without silver spoons," quipped Robert Reich.[6]

By amplifying their power through campaign contributions and super PACs, mega-contributions drown out what little voice and voting power ordinary citizens have in our democracy. Titans on the right and left are duking it out, like gladiators in the Roman Colosseum. Historian Peter Turchin's concept of "intra-elite competition," where wealthy people contest a limited number of political seats, is troublingly accurate. The non-wealthy majority is relegated to spectatorship from the cheap seats.

Increasingly, you may find a billionaire on your ballot, as a growing number decide they are uniquely qualified to run for office. At the global level, one study found that roughly 11 percent of billionaires have sought political office.[7] Study co-author Daniel Krcmaric writes, "While billionaires informally wield influence 'behind the scenes' via campaign contributions, media manipulation and social ties with politicians, it's striking how many billionaires themselves seek and hold formal political offices."[8] The study found that only 3.7 percent of U.S. billionaires have sought office, below the global average but still highly overrepresented for a small slice of the population. The more autocratic the society, the higher the percentage of billionaire candidates. And even when the candidates aren't billionaires, they are probably millionaires, like most U.S. members of Congress.[9]

OUR "BUY-PARTISAN" SYSTEM

Competition for billionaire patrons is strong in both the Democratic and Republican parties, such that these donors now act as de facto party bosses. As Dan Balz writes in the *Washington Post,* "Super-wealthy individuals receive outsize attention in presidential politics. And virtually every prospective candidate wants the support of a well-funded super PAC and the vocal backing of the mega rich. The disaffection of a disenchanted billionaire is treated as bad news for any candidate."[10] And that's just the money we know about. There are now back channels for dark money—anonymous giving that circumvents the campaign finance disclosure systems that have been put in place.

This system works very well for Upper Richistanis and their corporate servants. Spending on political influence is effectively one of the best investments the superrich can make, more lucrative than Berkshire Hathaway stock and pork belly futures. One study found that the "economic value of a $1 contribution in terms of lower state corporate taxes is approximately $6.65."[11]

Under the 2017–20 Trump presidency, these returns on political investments were even more dazzling. The Koch family spent $20 million lobbying for the 2017 Trump tax cut that personally saved them $1.4 billion.[12] With investments like these, it is no wonder the system is awash in influence funds.

THE WEALTH PRIMARY

The first stage of billionaire political capture is what some legal scholars describe as the "wealth primary."[13] Long before a candidate stands before voters for election in a party primary, the field has been winnowed by wealthy donors who cast their donation votes. Candidates without support from wealthy donors are not considered serious contenders and usually don't make the cut. As a result, candidates who strongly favor taxing the rich or regulating corporate power—red flags for the billionaire donor class—have a difficult time making it past this first hurdle.

In the early stage of the 2024 presidential election, a wealthy self-financed presidential candidate, North Dakota governor Doug Burgum, had a novel approach to attract attention. To qualify to be part of the 2024 Republican presidential debates, candidates had to demonstrate a minimum level of popularity measured by strength in public polls and numbers of individual donors. Burgum had donated a lot of his personal money to his campaign, so he didn't have enough individual donors to qualify for the debate. Burgum's work-around was to offer $20 gas cards to any new donors who gave $1 to his campaign. In this way, Burgum bought his inclusion in the first two presidential debates of 2023.[14]

Money isn't everything, but it usually calls the shots. Candidates for office still must run campaigns, connect with potential constituents, hone their message, and make their case to voters. But the biggest campaign donors, especially those in races that depend on buying expensive television ads, had "the best seats at the table of democracy in this year," in the words of Dan Balz.[15]

FOLLOW THE MONEY

In the 2024 Presidential race, with Donald Trump facing off against Kamala Harris, 150 billionaire families donated at least $1.9 billion combined to PACs and super PACs as of October 29, 2024.[16] These 150 families are worth over $2.67 trillion combined, and their political giving and influence are probably greatly understated, as they are masters of dark money and indirect means of giving. More than two-thirds (72 percent) of the contributions went to support Republican candidates, whereas fewer than a quarter (22 percent) went to Democrats (the remaining 6 percent went to Robert F. Kennedy Jr.'s presidential campaign and other candidates). Even within these 150 dynastically wealthy families, a few stand out, such as the Kochs, the Mellons, and the Adelsons. These three families contributed a total of at least $352 million.[17]

MONEY RULES AND LEGISLATES

Once the billionaire-friendly candidates have been elected, they do the real work of advancing an agenda that serves billionaire interests. Political scientists Ben Page and Martin Gilens have studied the long-term impact of the influence of the wealthy on legislating. Their basic conclusion is that the wealthy exercise disproportionate influence on what legislation passes and doesn't pass. The wealthy are particularly successful at blocking policies, even those that are broadly popular with most voters.

Page and Gilens analyzed two thousand federal policy decisions over twenty years and found that average U.S. voters, even when represented by a majoritarian interest group, had almost no influence in shaping public policy priorities. In their words, non-wealthy voters have "only a miniscule, near-zero, statistically non-significant impact upon public policy."[18] The only time average citizens see policy gains is when billionaires or their interest groups also support the policy.

On the other hand, economic elites, and their business-oriented interest groups, wield tremendous influence and effective veto power. "The public is often thwarted through *inaction,*" Page said in an interview. "The wealthy and partisan extremists often succeed at stopping proposals that are popular."[19] When you hear someone complain about gridlock and dysfunctional government, remind them that the billionaires have paid good money for this political paralysis.

The consequences have meaning for the non-wealthy. "Millions of Americans are denied government help with jobs, incomes, health care or retirement pensions," Gilens said in an interview with the *Washington Post.* "They do not get action against climate change or stricter regulation of the financial sector or a tax system that asks the wealthy to pay a fair share. On all these issues, wealthy Americans tend to want very different things than average Americans do. And the wealthy usually win."[20]

DARK MONEY AND THE SUPREME COURT

The Supreme Court's 2010 decision, *Citizens United v. Federal Election Commission,* opened the spigots of corporate and dark money. The court's ruling allows individuals or corporations to spend unlimited amounts on political advertising and other election-related activities, so long as the funds are not given directly to a candidate or a political party.[21] The creature emanating from the decision—the so-called super PAC—now funds the lion's share of political ads in federal elections and maintains the legal fiction that donations are not controlled by any particular party or politician or subject to coordination between the super PAC and the campaign.[22] Super PACs and anonymous dark money groups spent more than $9 billion on federal elections between 2010 and 2023, 30 percent from secret donors.[23]

The billionaires are not only capturing and corrupting the legislative branch but have spent billions to shift our Supreme Court to the right. Conservative judicial activists like Leonard Leo, co-chair of the Federalist Society, an influential network of conservative lawyers, have raised millions from billionaires. This includes a $1.6 billion donation from billionaire Barry Seid, possibly the largest political donation in history.[24] Funds have been channeled through donor-advised funds (DAFs) that have no disclosure requirements (and are thus known as "dark money") to advocacy groups working to influence the composition of the courts at all levels. This has resulted in the elimination of the federal right to abortion and to rulings rolling back environmental regulation, and numerous other harms.[25] Billionaires have also been providing huge in-kind contributions to individual Supreme Court Justices like Clarence Thomas, who has traveled the world on billionaire friend Harlan Crow's private jet and yachts and stayed at his secluded private resorts.[26]

PITIFUL FAILURE OF CAMPAIGN FINANCE REFORM

Election reformers have worked valiantly over many decades to limit the influence of wealthy donors on our campaign and political system. Different campaign finance laws have passed the U.S. Congress to require timely disclosure and/or cap the amount of donations that individuals can make to candidates and their campaigns.

One attempt at campaign finance reform was to create a system of federal matching funds to match smaller contributions from individuals. In exchange for accepting spending limits, candidates could receive federal funds. But since 2012, finalist presidential candidates of both major parties have opted out of this system, instead pursuing individual fundraising from wealthy donors to gain an electoral advantage.[27]

Federal laws currently cap the amount that individuals can donate to candidates to $3,300 for primaries and an additional $3,300 for a general election. But to circumvent these limits, the billionaires bundle their gifts, with children and grandchildren all maxing out donations made in their names. But more troubling, the wealthy donate to super PACs that have no limits and allow for anonymous contributions.

The rich don't always win. There are heartening and rare examples where votes still beat dollars in politics. In the 2016 election, candidates Bernie Sanders and Donald Trump both tapped into large pools of small donors giving $10, $15, or $20 to their campaigns. And self-financed billionaires and centimillionaire candidates who run for office don't always win. Voters often reject candidates who appear to be personally buying a seat in government.[28]

But the billionaires do win often enough to constitute a subversion of democracy. All these noble campaign financial reform efforts to limit the nexus between billionaire wealth and political influence have merely slowed the deluge of cash. Political money is like water running down a hill. Any effort to limit its flow eventually diverts it to another channel.

PROTECTING OUR DEMOCRACY FROM THE BILLIONAIRES

One answer to the problem of billionaire influence is laws to limit excessive wealth. To be clear, this is not "taxing the rich" for the purposes of raising revenue but to save democracy from plutocratic capture. The most important thing we can do to save our democracy is rewire the economy and tax system so as not to concentrate wealth and power in so few hands. But we also need rules to limit the influence of money and politics and restore the power and voice of ordinary voters, described in the following paragraphs.

FIXES

Legislative fixes are straightforward, although hardly easy to accomplish in a system rife with billionaire influence.

* **HR 1 For the People Act** is a comprehensive legislative package aimed at strengthening democracy protections and anti-corruption reforms. It would reduce the dominance of big money in politics by capping donations, strengthening disclosure, strengthening safeguards against foreign interference, and expanding ethics rules, while making it easier to vote in federal elections, and eliminating congressional gerrymandering.[29]

* **Public Financing of Elections**. As we've noted, many candidates opt out of the flawed federal system public financing, choosing to ignore the spending limits it imposes to raise more money from private donors. HR 1 would update the system of matching public funds and enable more candidates to run without being dependent on wealthy donors. Instead of matching private contributions one to one, it would match every dollar from a private donor, up to $200, with $6 in public financing, capped at $1,200. Billionaires would still attempt to throw their weight around, but more "billionaire-free" candidates would stand a chance.

* **Donor Disclosure**. Lawmakers could close avenues for secret dark money contributions by requiring

donor disclosure to 501(c)(4) corporations, currently one of the loopholes in the donor transparency system.

* **Democracy Vouchers**. In Seattle, all registered voters are given $100 in "democracy vouchers" that can be contributed to local candidates in city elections.[30]

Every four years, you are implored to vote, vote, vote—with endless reminders that this is a civic obligation. And while voting does still matter in some state and local elections, it is essential that we fight to reclaim our voice and votes from the billionaires.

CHAPTER 10

FOUR OTHER WAYS THE BILLIONAIRES ARE MESSING WITH YOUR LIFE

We've zeroed in on a few areas where billionaire disruption is acutely warping your life: the environment, housing, health care, voting power. Here I discuss briefly four additional examples of billionaire disruption.

HOW BILLIONAIRES ARE WARPING NONPROFITS AND PHILANTHROPY

The quality of our lives depends a great deal on the work of the independent nonprofit sector that strengthens our communities and contributes to a flourishing civic life—think your local YMCA, senior community center, after-school program, and arts or film festival. Whether providing critical human services, supporting education, or enabling arts and culture programming, the nonprofit sector depends on both tax dollars from government and the generous contributions of individuals, through an IRS regime that exempts those charities—and their donors—from paying taxes on monies raised or donated.

In the United States, the nonprofit sector accounts for 12.8 million jobs or roughly 10 percent of the labor force, equivalent in size to the U.S. manufacturing workforce.[1] In some states like West Virginia, North Dakota, and Pennsylvania, the nonprofit sector is even larger, accounting for more than 15 percent of the workforce.

Under the present system, ordinary taxpayers effectively subsidize the private power and influence of the billionaire class through a tax-exempt structure that was originally intended to strengthen the civic sector and promote the common good. However, billionaires' charity is not subject to any test of the "common good," other than that the organization has been certified by the IRS as a qualified nonprofit charity. The organization doesn't even need to be working on behalf of causes within the United States. That allows charitable giving of billionaires to be highly idiosyncratic—giving millions in what would otherwise be taxable revenue to preserve African wildlife, or to advocate for government funding of private rather than public schools.

Billionaire Generosity?

But aren't billionaires giving generously to charities to solve urgent world problems? You might get this impression from the regular pronouncements by benevolent billionaires about their philanthropy and good works. We've seen the mountain of publicity from Jeff Bezos and Mark Zuckerberg proclaiming that someday they will give away the bulk of their fortunes.[2] And more than 244 billionaires from thirty countries have taken the Giving Pledge, an initiative founded by Warren Buffett, Melinda French Gates, and Bill Gates to increase charitable giving by the extremely wealthy.[3] And indeed, a few are moving significant money, like MacKenzie Scott, the ex-wife of Jeff Bezos, who has given over $17.3 billion in her pledge to "empty the vault," reducing her fortune from its 2022 peak of $56 billion to $29.4 billion.[4] And the inspiration for the Giving Pledge, Chuck Feeney, gave away over $9 billion and died no longer a billionaire, his stated goal.[5]

With hundreds of billionaires pledging to give away half their wealth by the time of their death, we would presumably see billionaire fortunes decline. But on the tenth anniversary of the Giving Pledge, in 2020, researchers found that the total net worth of the sixty-two living initial pledgers hadn't diminished at all. In fact, it had nearly *doubled,* when adjusted for inflation.[6] Elon Musk signed the Giving Pledge in 2012 when he joined the Forbes billionaire list. As of New Year's Day 2025, his wealth had increased to over $428 billion.[7] Part of the challenge is that billionaire wealth is simply rising so fast—U.S. billionaires have seen their total wealth increase more than $4 trillion since 2020.[8]

While billionaires do of course still donate directly to charities, grand philanthropic pledges are often fulfilled by dumping funds into family foundations or donor-advised funds (DAFs) that could exist in perpetuity. Some 41 percent of charitable donations now flow through intermediaries like these, outpacing direct donations to many traditional charities.[9]

Billionaires claim enormous tax deductions for parking funds in these intermediaries. But there's little to no guarantee that money will ever make it to working charities.[10] Foundations are required to pay out only 5 percent of their assets each year, and most dole out just slightly more than this minimum.

DAFs face no annual payout requirement *at all*. Lax reporting requirements make it difficult to assess their activity, but recent reports suggest that median DAF payouts are shockingly low.[11] Bottom line: Don't be waiting for the billionaires to step up and solve the critical problems of our day.

Top-Heavy Philanthropy: Dollars Up and Donors Down

The expansion of charitable giving by fat cat donors, while ostensibly helpful to nonprofit organizations, is in some ways undermining their long-term sustainability. Mirroring the four-decade-long rise of the billionaire class, philanthropic giving in the United States has become more "top-heavy," with a steady decline in small donor giving over the last few decades.[12] This troubling trend has been masked by a rise in charitable giving by the very wealthy, a development that makes nonprofit groups now more dependent on fewer wealthy donors rather than broad support from many middle-income donors.

A fundraiser for a nonprofit organization in the 1970s or 1980s probably worked with the "80/20 rule," which surmised that charity received 80 percent of its donations from 20 percent of its donors.[13] Under this assumption, it made sense that nonprofit fundraisers worked to attract major donors but also maintained a broad base of smaller donor support that balanced out revenue. But what if the reality is now 98/2 percent, with 98 percent of nonprofits' donations coming from one or two large donors? It makes the organization vulnerable to closure if that donor suddenly dies, moves on to another cause, or loses his or her money. The collapse of Bernie Madoff's investment scheme in 2008, along with its profits from what was ultimately a Ponzi scheme, had far-reaching ripple effects through the nonprofit world, when donations from billionaires invested with his firm suddenly disappeared.

Subsidizing the Pet Projects of Billionaires

The United States has a unique system of tax-incentivized charitable giving, providing generous tax breaks to those who donate to qualified working charities.[14] But this has become skewed in large part due to the 2017 tax reforms that raised the personal exemption for charitable giving, greatly reducing the percentage of households that now itemize their deductions to under 10 percent.[15] Under the current system, the wealthier the donor, the greater the tax break for the charitable deduction. This is because billionaire donors reduce not only their income taxes when giving to charity, but also their estate, gift, and capital gains taxes. For every dollar that a billionaire gives to charity, the Treasury effectively chips in up to 74 cents in reduced tax revenue.[16] The remaining non-wealthy taxpayers effectively subsidize the private giving priorities of the very wealthy.

The billionaires are distorting the charitable landscape by dictating the destination of billions a year in charitable donations. This is wealth that would have been taxed and dispersed as public investments. Unlike government spending that is subject to a democratic process and oversight of distribution, charitable giving often operates as a form of private power,

"Yes, we're a charity tackling skyrocketing income inequality, but we're also a charity that should be saying 'I love my billionaire funder.'"

reflecting the whims and biases of a small slice of wealthy donors. And as you might suspect, billionaires give to different causes than do average citizens.[17] The billionaire class is more inclined to give large legacy donations to universities, hospitals, and museums that are set up to woo big donors and to offer them perks like naming rights.[18]

The wealthy also give differently in another way, as mentioned in the discussion of the Giving Pledge. Instead of giving directly to working charities that service needy people on the ground, like the Boys and Girls Clubs or a food bank, they increasingly give to intermediaries that they fully control, such as private family foundations and DAFs.[19]

The "wealth defense industry" of financial advisers and wealth managers—the same characters helping billionaires hide their wealth and reduce their tax bills—has gotten into the business of promoting DAFs and private foundations as tax-advantaged giving vehicles that allow immediate tax breaks but require little payout and transparency.[20] Some financial advisers are incentivized to encourage donors to place funds in DAFs so that the donors will retain them as investment advisers. This, of course, further discourages a timely payout of funds to charitable causes.[21]

There is now $1.75 *trillion* in charitable funds warehoused in these intermediaries, with only a minimal amount of dollars dribbling out.[22]

STRAIGHTFORWARD FIXES

I've been part of several efforts to reform these rules to protect the nonprofit sector and our democracy from billionaire-dominated philanthropy.[23] We're pushing for legislation to increase the required foundation payout to 7 percent and improve transparency, so the public knows where donated funds are going. There's also a proposal to mandate DAFs to have requirements to pay out funds in a timely way and disclose where donations are going. A more far-reaching reform would be to cap the deduction for charitable donations so billionaires can't so easily opt out of paying taxes. We could also expand a tax credit for low- and middle-income givers. The basic principle is simple: if you get a deduction for charitable giving, you must actually *contribute to a working charity.*

HOW BILLIONAIRES DECIDE WHAT'S FOR DINNER

Billionaires are doing your menu planning and raising your grocery bill.

A small number of billionaire "food barons" are dictating what's on your dinner plate. They are shaping where and how your food is produced, its cost, and its nutritional value. Today, a handful of global companies dominate the food system, wielding tremendous power and monopoly market share. They effectively exercise economic dominance over farmers, growers, and other suppliers in the communities where they operate, shrinking those producers' profit margins in favor of their own. Their supersized, industrial model of agricultural production contributes to frightening new forms of pollution and climate-altering greenhouse gases.

In fewer than twenty years, the rapid consolidation of food companies has minted dozens of new "food baron" billionaires. With their increasing power, these food barons have extracted trillions in value from customers, workers, farmers, and taxpayers. Austin Frerick, who grew up in the Iowa farm belt, chronicles these trends in his book, *Barons: Money, Power, and the Corruption of America's Food Industry.* Frerick writes that the U.S. food "supply chain—everything from seeds to baby formula—has fallen under the control of a narrow group of individuals, leaving family farmers and local businesses fighting an uphill battle just to stay in business. Although economic concentration affects many industries, there are few areas where it is more prevalent, or where it more directly affects people, than the food system." Frerick identifies seven major food barons who dominate their sectors.[24] What follows are a few highlights.

The Hog Barons

The dominant powerhouses in pork production are Jeff and Deb Hansen, owners of Iowa Select Farms, a company that employs 7,400 people, including contractors. Iowa Select has changed the physical landscape of Iowa, increasing the number of concentrated animal feeding operations, or CAFOs, essentially massive lots raising thousands of hogs (or other livestock). The number of such feedlots owned by Iowa Select has increased fivefold over the past twenty years, leading to the collapse of smaller hog farms.[25] As Austin Frerick writes, "CAFOs generate colossal amounts of manure waste, forming gargantuan anerobic lagoons that foul the air, pollute local water supplies around the farm, and contributing to antibiotic resistance among their animals."[26] Iowa is now home to a third of all hogs raised in the United States, with an estimated thirteen thousand CAFO confinement operations. Meanwhile, the vibrant rural communities that supported diversified family farms have suffered.

Iowa Select has used its considerable clout to block environmental regulations and laws in Iowa. "Iowa Select became a behemoth as the result of decades of deregulation that allowed power to concentrate in our food system," said Frerick. "And it's not just smelly. It's a sad story of the corporate capture of my home state."

Meanwhile, the Hansens, worth $270 million according to Wealth-X, travel from their gated home in Des Moines to their coastal retreat in Florida on a private jet emblazoned with the phrase "When Pigs Fly."

The Grain Barons

The largest privately owned company in the United States, Cargill-MacMillan, dominates a *quarter* of the world's grain trade.[27] At least one hundred family members together own an estimated 88 percent of the company, which rules markets in corn, soy, and other commodity grains. They are one of the wealthiest family dynasties in the United States, with $60.6 billion in assets; twenty-one individual family members are billionaires, according to *Forbes*.[28] The extended family is one of the billionaire clans that have dynasty trusts formed in the state of South Dakota, one of our country's notorious tax havens.[29]

Cargill-MacMillan operates much like the great Standard Oil monopoly did, through vertical integration: grow the grain, store it, move it, process it, and distribute. They have bought up competition and consolidated their market power. This consolidation squeezes farmers to accept lower prices for their crops, as they have fewer potential buyers to sell to. This is one reason why the share of each food dollar that goes to farmers has shrunk from 53¢ in 1946 to 15¢ today.[30]

Cargill-MacMillan has deployed its market power and political lobbying to shape food policy, particularly through the federal Farm Bill, which allocates huge subsidies to the agricultural sector. They've lobbied to ensure the number one use of corn is for ethanol fuel; and for massive subsidies for corn and high fructose corn syrup, which has undercut traditional sugar produced from beets and sugarcane. Meanwhile, we are seeing a worldwide epidemic of type 2 diabetes, highly correlated in peer-reviewed science research with the consumption of soft drinks sweetened with high fructose corn syrup.[31] In response, Cargill-MacMillan has funded front groups to advance studies disputing negative health consequences of corn syrup, sowing doubt in science and distorting policy decision-making.

One way the billionaire food barons conceal their vast power is through ownership of many seemingly independent companies and brands. The coffee barons are especially effective at this. Have you ever gone to one of these establishments? Peet's Coffee, Caribou Coffee, Einstein Bros. Bagels, Bruegger's Bagels, Manhattan Bagel, Noah's New York Bagels, Krispy Kreme, Pret A Manger, Insomnia Cookies, and Panera Bread. They are *all* owned by one food conglomerate, the German-based JAB Holding Company, controlled by the billionaire Reimann family, worth an estimated $5.6 billion, according to *Forbes*.[32] Maybe you think you are buying coffee from a neighborhood café, like Stumptown Coffee Roasters, La Colombe Coffee Roasters, Intelligentsia Coffee, or Green Mountain Coffee. All these brands—including the Keurig coffee maker you use at home—are owned by JAB Holding, which sells more coffee annually than Starbucks.

JAB Holding operates like a private equity company in their acquisition strategy. "JAB bought companies directly, focusing on rolling up as many firms as possible in the same industry and then combining them into one new megafirm," writes Austin Frerick. "The next step was to restructure the firms they had purchased, which likely entailed realizing as many 'efficiencies' as possible . . . [and] often involves a combination of layoffs and leveraging of size and market power to squeeze suppliers and the workers that remain."[33]

You can also find billionaire food barons dominating the dairy, berry, and meat sectors. Today half of all milk is produced by 3 percent of farms, with the Indiana-based Fair Oaks Farm leading the way. Driscoll's dominates the berry market through a contract market system that is known for its notorious labor practices.[34] They don't actually grow any berries but contract with 750 growers in two dozen countries, indirectly employing more than 100,000 workers. "The off-shoring of the American food system has made our food more like the rest of the American economy: uniform, lackluster in quality, and highly consolidated," writes Austin Frerick. "This restructuring is visible in every aisle of the grocery store. Eaters get a lower-quality, blander product."

The Barons of Beef

The "slaughter barons" are led by the billionaire Batista family, with estimated wealth of $5.8 billion. The Batistas own JBS, a company built on bribes and corruption in Brazil and now in the United States. On a given day, JBS slaughters 76,550 cattle, 127,100 hogs, and 13.8 million birds. JBS sold more food in 2021 than Nestlé, PepsiCo, Kraft Heinz, and Unilever.[35] Like other food barons, JBS relies on the contract model, which drives down labor costs, squeezes producers, and dominates market distribution channels. Thanks to massive deforestation in the Amazon region, where many trees and vegetables are cleared to make way for its cattle ranches, JBS's carbon footprint is the size of Italy's.

The Grocer Barons

Selling the food are the grocer barons, led by Walmart, 50 percent owned by the dynastically wealthy Walton family, worth an estimated $349.3 billion.[36] Walmart sells a third of all groceries in the United States, a stark contrast from 1997 when only 21 percent of all groceries were purchased through the four largest grocery chains. As Walmart's market share grew over the last two decades, more than twenty-five other grocery chains went bankrupt, leading to the closure of thirteen thousand local grocery stores in a decade. Your local grocer—the Mr. Hooper of Sesame Street—is no more.

Walmart's dominance of the grocery market is unprecedented. The closest comparison was in 1933 when A&P had 16 percent of the market. This concentration led to an urgent anti-monopoly reform movement to rein in anticompetitive processes. Between 1925 and 1937, state legislatures introduced nearly a thousand bills to break up A&P's monopoly power, of which fifty were enacted. Today, by contrast, federal and state governments are failing to use their regulatory power to break up consolidation within the food sector.[37]

As Austin Frerick writes, "Rather than working to limit concentrated power, politicians in both parties have either helped entrench powerful interests or attempted to conduct policy in a manner that is agnostic to power."[38] Unless there is a dramatic shift toward antitrust enforcement, we can look forward to further consolidation of the food sector.

BILLIONAIRES ARE EXPLOITING YOUR LOVE OF FIDO

The billionaires know you love your furry family members, and they'd like to profit from your affection.

Have you had to seek veterinary attention for a beloved pet in recent years? Have you noticed higher costs for vaccines and routine exams? Do you occasionally need a pet sitter and wish to purchase services from an online service? I've got bad news for you: the billionaires have fixed their sights on you and on every corner of the pet care economy, with the goal of squeezing more money out of you.

Pet ownership was on the rise even before the COVID-19 pandemic; today roughly 70 percent of U.S. households have at least one pet. The share of household income spent on pets has risen significantly, with an estimated $123 billion in 2021. While pet insurance is available, few pet owners have it. Yet many are willing to take on enormous debt for high-priced medical services. In a recent article in the *New York Times* about the rising cost of pet care, Katie Thomas writes, "A generation ago, pet owners with a seriously ill animal may have had little choice but to opt for euthanasia if they wanted to relieve their pet's suffering. Now, they must choose between extending the animal's life and going into what can be debilitating debt or letting an animal die."

Thomas spoke to pet owners who were still paying off credit card debt years after their animals had died. She reports that animal welfare groups are finding pet owners relinquishing their animals to shelters when they can't afford veterinary bills.[39]

For many people, their relationships with animals are more steadfast than their connections with humans. With a growing percentage of people saying they have only one or two people they can depend on, if any, the unconditional love of a pet plays an important role in our lives.[40] "Pets are filling a gap," observed Greg Hartmann, CEO of Veterinary Centers of America (rebranded as "VCA"), one of the largest for-profit veterinary medical enterprises. He noted that young adults are waiting until later in life to get married and have children, if they have children at all. "We're seeing now the younger generation, millennial and Gen Z, own nearly half of the pets in the United States, and their spending behaviors seem to be outpacing the preceding generations."[41]

These trends have not been lost on billionaire wealth extractors, who are looking for the opportunities to siphon income off every corner of the pet-provisioning sector. As a result, there has been an unprecedented concentration of ownership over the last decade in pet food, pet stores, and veterinary care, and pet services, like Rover.com. The biggest players in the pet economy include dynastic billionaire families like the Mars candy clan and the German Reimann family (JAB Holding Company), along with billionaire-backed private equity firms that are snatching up companies in the pet sector.

Veterinary Care

One of the most startling areas of consolidation is in veterinary care. An estimated 25 percent of all general veterinary services are now owned by billionaires and private equity firms, up from 5 percent a decade ago. And the wealth aggregators own an estimated 75 percent of specialty veterinary clinics and hospitals, the most profitable segment of the sector.[42] It is no coincidence that over the last decade, the cost of veterinary care has risen by more than 60 percent, dramatically outpacing inflation.[43] I suspect this is largely due to the impact of private investor consolidation in the sector.

The single biggest owner of pet care products is the Mars family, the third-generation candy-making dynasty worth an estimated $130 billion, making them the second wealthiest family in the United States after the Waltons of Walmart.[44] The Mars family and their notoriously secretive, privately held company own 2,500 pet-care facilities including BluePearl and Veterinary Centers of America (VCA). They also own several pet-food companies, an online pet pharmacy, and a kitty-litter company.[45]

The second-largest consolidator of pet health care is National Veterinary Associates, or NVA, with 1,100 clinics and hospitals. They are known for buying up local mom-and-pop practices and keeping the same name, signage, and veterinarians—such that you may not know that your pet care is coming from a global conglomerate. NVA is owned by the Reimann family, whom we met in the discussion of billionaire food barons, the second-richest family in Germany and owners of JAB Holding Company.[46]

As with human health care, billionaire consolidators aim to extract big coin on veterinary services, pushing expensive tests and pricey interventions, instituting aggressive billing and collection, and focusing on cost cutting on the service side, including squeezing wages from employees.

Four major private equity buyouts of veterinary care operations occurred in the first half of 2024. Billionaires and their private equity firms are interested in these businesses because they are high in consumer demand, largely cash pay, and buffered from the business cycle—along with historically being a less regulated corner of health care.[47] These vulture investors typically collect management fees on all transactions, strip out profitable assets (including real estate), call the shots in terms of major decision-making in the practice, and charge fees for monitoring them, even as some of the companies they acquire spiral into bankruptcy. "It's like setting the fire, being paid to put out the fire, and collecting the insurance on the fire all at the same time," quipped Stephen Dubner, host of *Freakonomics Radio*.[48]

Consolidation and the monopoly power it produces allows a smaller number of pet care providers to raise prices and suppress wages for veterinary workers, especially in localities without a lot of choices of provider.

Pet Services like Dog Walking and Sitters

My friend Katherine earns a little extra income walking dogs. Recently she started finding clients through an online platform called Rover.com. "Rover takes 20 percent for making the match," Katherine told me. "They're just an app, taking a fifth of my earnings. And they charge the pet owner an 11 percent booking fee, capped at $50." Rover charges a pet care provider $49 to put a profile up on their account. In addition to matchmaking, Rover offers a guarantee to both parties and backup insurance, claiming in their motto, "We're here for you." But when Katherine encountered a dangerous dog situation—and reached out with some urgency—the company failed to respond to requests for help. "Meanwhile, the person providing services is on the hook for any liabilities," Katherine said, sharing the fine print of the service agreement. "Rover absolves itself of responsibility for just about everything. Pet owner and service provider beware."[49]

In November 2023, the billionaire-backed private equity firm Blackstone, with more than $1 trillion in assets, acquired Rover for $2.3 billion in cash. They see nothing but growth in the pet care space.[50]

Katherine went on to describe the cost of veterinary care for her late dog, Princess Lucy. "You walk into that clinic, and they swipe your credit card, and you know you won't be walking out of there for less than $1,000 and probably much more." And let's not even talk about pet stores and pet food. The 1,500-store Petco company is owned by the Luxembourg-based private equity firm CVC Capital Partners. And an estimated 95 percent of the common pet food brands are owned by six global conglomerates, with number one being the Mars family, followed by Nestlé Purina, Smucker's, Colgate-Palmolive, Diamond, and General Mills.

Be careful what you love, because the billionaires are paying attention; they will figure out how to siphon as much of what you're willing to spend on your passion as they can.

BILLIONAIRES ARE PROFITING FROM THE ULTIMATE CAPTIVE MARKET: PRISONS

The billionaires love investments in captive markets where consumers have no choice but to pay high prices for their products and services. It thus stands to reason that several have focused on squeezing income from people in prison and their families. As of 2023, there were more than 1.2 million people behind bars in federal and state prisons and in local jails.[51]

Private equity firms have horned in on the market for prison telecommunications, prison health, and food services in particular. As Derek Seidman writes in *Truthout*, "The lack of oversight around private equity, combined with the sector's predatory tactics, has created a nightmare for captive prison populations, whose most basic needs are subjected to the whims of investors. Not surprisingly, this has produced numerous scandals and mounting lawsuits."[52]

Billionaires have extracted huge profits from prisoner communications, where private equity owns roughly 90 percent of the incarcerated market. Billionaire Tom Gores (with $9.1 billion according to *Forbes*) is one of the largest prison profiteers. He chairs Platinum Equity, a massive private equity firm, and also owns the Detroit Pistons basketball team.[53] Platinum owns a company called Securus and a subsidiary, JPay, that charge prisoners inflated fees to access email, games, and e-books. During the pandemic, they provided tablets to prisoners in New York State while charging for emails and downloads of free books. In 2021, they were fined $6 million for requiring prisoners to pay fees to access *their own money.*[54]

Some states and regulators are waking up to these horrific abuses. The California Public Utilities Commission finally regulated calling rates in detention facilities, capping the rate per minute that these predatory corporations could charge incarcerated people and their family members. But due to deregulation of utilities over the last several decades, prison telecom firms have moved into other markets important to prisoners, such as gaming and direct messaging. As Kalena Thomhave writes, "Prison telecoms aren't shy about touting such unregulated communications as video calling as new revenue streams; they're part of their pitch to potential investors. When the FCC steps in to regulate video calling and further regulate phone calls, it's likely that prison telecoms will expand their electronic messaging and other services."[55] The billionaire predators stay one step ahead of the regulators, extracting wealth where they can.

* * * *

THERE ARE PLENTIFUL additional examples of sectors of society that are burned by billionaires. These include billionaires deciding what we consume for news, and how much it costs to die and have a funeral. The billionaires are moving into student debt processing and shaping what you pay to park in many cities. Every day I awaken to new ways the billionaire class is disrupting our lives and livelihoods. Once you start to see it, you, too, will be making these connections.

Part Three

PROTECTING YOURSELF AND YOUR COMMUNITY FROM THE BILLIONAIRE BURN

The rise of the billionaire class is the result of an economy rigged to pump wealth to a few thousand households, with sadly tragic disruptions to the lives of everyday Americans.

There are at least two reasons why we tolerate these extreme inequalities. First, there are powerful narratives that justify the billionaires siphoning up a huge amount of society's wealth. People believe these narratives enough to excuse them or blame themselves. The second reason is that the problem feels intractable: the wealthy and their grip on policymakers are too powerful and entrenched to effect change. The last two chapters aim to address these important concerns.

CHAPTER 11

DISRUPTING THE NARRATIVES THAT JUSTIFY BILLIONAIRE WEALTH

A POWERFUL STORY JUSTIFIES OUR CURRENTLY ABSURD concentration of wealth. Distilled to a bumper sticker, this narrative is essentially: "People are where they deserve to be." In other words, the extremely wealthy deserve to be where they are due to hard work, intelligence, gumption, grit, risk taking, and so on. And by contrast, those who are poor or struggling are where they belong due to their *lack* of industry, intelligence, or creativity.

This story of deservedness (sometimes called "meritocracy") is the whopper mythology that binds the many individual facets of inequality together, making the continued acceleration of billionaire power and influence possible. It justifies the racial wealth divide, the growing wage disparities between owners and workers, and the rise of the billionaire class itself. The narrative shows up in both the personal stories people tell about themselves and the political narratives we tell about others.

This story of merit has historically been deployed by privileged and advantaged people to maintain and justify their dominant position and excessive rewards, excising in the telling the help and assistance they may have received from others in the form of family networks, inheritance, and government subsidies. It is the story that white people tell themselves to justify their racialized advantages over multiple generations. In the political arena, the deservedness narrative treats government subsidies for poor people, immigrants, and people of color as shameful and wasteful, and subsidies for billionaires as virtuous and prudent means of creating jobs and expanding the economy.

This story is of course a foundational component of the American Dream, the narrative that anyone who works hard enough in the United States can get ahead and become a millionaire. It is the story we are told in countless ways from a young age—the narrative tide we all swim in—made even more difficult to resist by its kernels of truth. Apart from the ways it serves power, it is a story that inspires many.

WHY NARRATIVE?

How do we change the deeply entrenched myth of deservedness that is used to rationalize billionaire wealth and justify inaction to reverse it? First, we must recognize that this myth is a boulder in the road on the journey to creating a more fair and equitable society. We must understand the ways that these narratives matter—and how they deflect us from focusing on the real solutions and fixes.

Facts appeal to the head, but stories touch our heart and soul. Facts lay out an accurate picture, but stories help people make sense of those facts. Our brains are constantly trying to rationalize—or reject—facts against larger narratives to help us make sense of the world.

Thus, to win a populace over to support measures to reduce billionaire power, it will be important to dislodge the story that Jeff Bezos deserves his billions, a fiction to which many people of all classes hold tight.

ACKNOWLEDGING INDIVIDUAL CONTRIBUTIONS WHILE DEBUNKING BILLIONAIRE MERITOCRACY NARRATIVES

Now, you may be thinking, don't most mythologies have a kernel of truth that enables a meta-myth to grow around it? After all, what individuals do in their lives does matter and does influence economic outcomes. And even within rigid caste systems, people often have some sliver of agency.

For example, it is true that people make enormous sacrifices of time, money, and stress to start their own businesses. They should be recognized, honored, and appropriately compensated for their efforts. But let's be clear: the incomprehensibly extreme levels of income and wealth inequality that we are seeing in this Second Gilded Age—the yawning racial wealth divide, the gargantuan gap between the bank balance of the average worker and the overflowing vault of the billionaire who employs him, cannot be attributed to differences in individual effort, or to profits earned through fair business practices, or to defensible rules of capital aggregation. These trends are instead the result of multigenerational advantage, systemic breaks reserved for elites, corporate greed, and brute power politics, delinked from individual choices and efforts.

When the oil industry magnate J. Paul Getty was once asked how you become wealthy, he replied that it was quite easy. There are three things you must do to become rich in America, he opined. First, get up early every morning. Second, work hard all day. Third, find oil. His implication, I think, is that there is some degree of blind luck in business.

When people hear statistics like "the richest 1 percent have 42 percent of all the wealth," or "800 U.S. billionaires own over $6 trillion," they may think: those people got up early, worked hard all day, and invented a better mousetrap or MS-DOS or a better social media platform to suck up hours of your day.

They may also be thinking of real people they know and stories they know to be true. They are thinking about Uncle Ed, the underemployed moocher who can't seem to hold a job for longer than three months and shows up empty-handed to Thanksgiving dinner. Or conversely about Aunt Kate, who hustles all week in her job, has two side businesses, and shows up with the full turkey and stuffing. One is a slacker, and the other is a go-getter. Perhaps they deserve different rewards in life?

The conversation about inequality is warped by such individual stories; people take their personal experiences of the Uncle Eds and Aunt Kates in their lives and project them onto national statistics about inequality like a ten-thousand-watt projector. Now, few would propose that Aunt Kate and Uncle Ed be paid the exact same salary. In a healthy equitable society, there will still be differences in salaries and standards of living based on personal characteristics, efforts, and choices. But should Kate earn five thousand times more? No, probably not. Should Kate have a private jet while those making the minimum wage in her business are consigned to living in their car?

And what if there is a more nuanced story behind their differences? What if Uncle Ed's service in the military left him suffering from trauma and addiction, leading to a downward spiral in health and well-being? Maybe he gives enormously to his community of veterans and is depleted when he shows up with this extended family. No one knows the whole story until they walk in someone's shoes.

Similarly, Elon Musk and his companies have developed and disseminated some useful technologies, and he should be recognized and rewarded for his effort. But is his personal contribution worth more than $400 billion, roughly the 2023 gross domestic product of Denmark? [1] In 1982, the ratio between the pay of average workers and that of the average CEOs of Fortune 500 companies was 42 to 1. And in many companies, the ratio was below 20 to 1. By 2015, the ratio was more than 300 to 1. Did CEOs in 2015 become appreciably more brilliant? Did they get up earlier, work significantly longer hours, and invent better rat traps? Nope. Their compensation is part of a system that overvalues some and undervalues others.

The good news is that the excesses of our age of inequality are beginning to sink in, with more and more Americans beginning to understand that the massive wealth of the titans of industry may be coming at their expense. A 2024 Harris Poll on public attitudes toward billionaires found that 60 percent of younger Americans believe "billionaires are making it harder to achieve my American dream," with 68 percent of Gen Z (ages eighteen to twenty-seven) believing that "billionaires are creating a more unfair society."[2]

TELL TRUE STORIES OF WEALTH AND ADVANTAGE

When we hear success narratives of the billionaires, we should acknowledge the laudable individual qualities that people bring to their enterprises. But we should also conduct an honest inventory of their wider web of supports—the matrix of public investments that creates the fertile ground for any enterprise or activity.

Ben Cohen and Jerry Greenfield, co-founders of Ben & Jerry's ice cream, are often considered successful entrepreneurs who have become very wealthy. But when they tell their success story, they include the help they got. "We started our enterprise with help from two state universities, the Small Business Administration and a Federal Urban Development Action Grant—all paid for by a previous generation of taxpayers," they wrote in *USA Today*. "Our company thrived thanks in part to scientific advances in agriculture, public roads and other infrastructure, intellectual property protections and a regulated marketplace where we could raise capital and ensure the quality of our ingredients. Someone else paid for these public systems that enabled our business to prosper."[3]

Journalists have a role to play in telling a truer story of corporate entrepreneurship. Instead of writing "great man" stories of wealth creators, which fill the business sections of bookstores and magazines, they ought to tell the larger picture of how social networks and public investment and subsidies aided their enterprises.

We can each do our part by thinking about the personal advantages we've profited from in our own lives. How we tell our own story of how we got where we are can serve as a role model to others and shift away from the narrative myth of individual achievement alone. Try telling your own "I didn't do it alone" story by recognizing the web of supports that all humans depend on. What help did we get along the way? Help from family, community, teachers, mentors? Did we get financial help from family, government, or community organizations?

Telling true stories of wealth and advantage can help shift these dynamics. Unless we change the narrative to a truer story, it will be difficult to win campaigns to rein in billionaire wealth and become a more just, prosperous, and thriving nation.

CHAPTER 12

AN AGENDA TO REDUCE BILLIONAIRE POWER AND IMPROVE OUR LIVES

IF BILLIONAIRES ARE A POLICY FAILURE, THEN WHAT IS a policy success? What policies might the United States adopt to thwart democracy-endangering concentrations of wealth?

The concentration of wealth in the billionaire class—and its resulting capture of our political system—seems like a tough nut to crack. We know that taxing extreme wealth is the most straightforward way to redistribute power and wealth, and in early chapters I described some high-priority tax reforms. We also know that breaking up monopoly power and reining in the excesses of billionaire-backed private equity funds is essential to prevent the kind of harmful extraction chronicled in this book.

In her book, *Limitarianism: The Case Against Extreme Wealth,* Dutch political philosopher Ingrid Robeyns argues we should put a cap on the superrich. Robeyns makes the case for a 100 percent tax on wealth exceeding $10 million. In tandem, she makes the case for policies that foster opportunity for the non-wealthy. "Our societies' key social and economic institutions should give people genuinely equal opportunities, through affordable childcare, free high-quality education and a comprehensive anti-poverty strategy."[1]

But such bold changes are theoretical fantasies without the broad-based political movement to claim more of the country's productivity for the masses who produced it. And that movement doesn't seem to be present in 2025. It was not that long ago, however, when Congress almost passed President Biden's "Build Back Better" agenda in 2022, a transformative program to invest $4 trillion over the next decade in climate mitigation, poverty alleviation, childcare, and much more. The legislation passed the U.S. House and came within two votes of passage in the Senate. The billionaires knew they needed to swing only two votes—Senators Joe Manchin (D-WV) and Kyrsten Sinema (D-AZ)—to block the legislation, and that's what they did. But it was so close! Joe Biden was the first U.S. president to press for a tax on billionaires and a levy on private jet fuel. All these policies were wildly popular with majorities of Democrats, Independents, and Republicans.

The way forward is to press for big policy ideas that will meaningfully improve people's lives while working to unrig the rules that benefit billionaires. Reducing inequality will require new rules and policies that lift the income floor for those at the bottom, broaden opportunity for everyone in the middle, and break up the overconcentration of wealth at the top. We need rule changes that rewire capitalism for shared prosperity for all rather than spoils for the few.[2]

CHANGES THAT LIFT THE FLOOR

Policies that "lift the floor" aim to establish a basic standard of material security—they reduce poverty by promoting a level of well-being that no one should be allowed to fall below. Many European social democracies have fewer billionaires and greater equality thanks to strong social safety nets and policies that maintain a high wage floor of income as well as standard health and basic services accessible to all. In the United States, by contrast, one-third of workers have no paid sick days, and fully one-half have no paid vacation days. Similarly, most workers in other OECD countries are members of unions or covered by blanket labor agreements. In the United States, notwithstanding encouraging signs of resurgence, decades of aggressive anti-union policies and practices have corroded the right to join a union and engage in collective bargaining.

Examples of rule changes that would lift people out of poverty, increase economic security for the precarious, and reduce inequality include the following:

Raise the Minimum Wage to a Living Wage

The federal minimum wage has not been increased since 2009, lagging inflation in basic living expenses in housing, health care, food, transportation, and childcare. Because of the rise in the cost of living, the current federal minimum wage ($7.25 per hour) has nearly 50 percent less buying power than it had when it was last raised in 2009. According to the Consumer Price Index, $7.25 in 2009 is roughly $10.61 in today's dollars.[3] The minimum wage for restaurant servers who receive tips has been stuck at $2.13 an hour since 1991.[4]

Provide True Universal Health Care

Our aim should be to expand health coverage so that every child and adult gets good basic health care—and so that no one is allowed to become sick, become destitute, or die because of lack of health care. The Affordable Care Act, now under threat of erosion, was a step toward universal coverage, increasing the number of those with health care by 20 million. But more than 26 million people, or 8 percent of the U.S. population, still lack coverage, primarily because of cost.[5] We need to work toward a system of "Medicare for all" or at least a publicly financed option for providing health care.

Strengthen the Right to Organize and Basic Labor Standards and Protections

Ensuring basic worker rights and standards can lift the bottom 40 percent of workers who are currently the most exploited and disadvantaged. The labor movement is advocating for strengthening the right to organize a union. Ensuring that every worker has a forty-hour workweek (or overtime pay), minimum paid vacation time, paid family medical and sick leave, and protections against wage theft would make life more humane and equal for everyone. And on the business side, improving people's lives would of course increase productivity.

Provide Access to Lifelong Learning and Job Retraining

Quality education, and the opportunity to continue education through one's lifetime, should be accessible to all. Especially in a global economy undergoing significant technological transitions, workers need to be able to reskill to keep their jobs or get new ones.

Provide Refundable Tax Credits and a Guaranteed Minimum Income (or Universal Basic Income)

One way to ensure a secure income floor is to pay out a minimum income to supplement low wages. Expanding the Earned Income Tax Credit—by many accounts, the most effective and easy way to administer an anti-poverty program in the United States—would be relatively simple.[6] There are dozens of pilots in the United States and around the world exploring the impact of a guaranteed income and other social welfare guarantees.[7]

Provide Government Employment as Last Resort

A key policy that honors the dignity and importance of work is making the public sector an employer of last resort for those who cannot find a job in the private sector. Like the Works Progress Administration during the 1930s Great Depression, the government should identify useful work that the private sector is not doing—and pay unemployed or underemployed Americans decent wages to do it. Like many public expenditures, this could be paid for through budget allocations or a dedicated tax. Such projects could accompany investments in crumbling infrastructure and climate resilience projects.

Furnish Adequate Welfare Support

Those kept from working by disability, mental or physical illness, or age need a social welfare safety net composed of many of the services described previously. Currently, disability benefits are greatly inadequate and consign many to a life of poverty.[8] In addition, a better safety net could help some return to the paid labor force by stabilizing their housing, health, and care tasks.

Policies that raise the floor not only reduce poverty and economic deprivation; they also reduce economic insecurity and stress throughout society. Until stricken ourselves, we greatly underestimate how easily and rapidly job loss, divorce, or major illness can lead to destitution, homelessness, and death—and how many Americans have experienced such instability.

RULE CHANGES THAT REDUCE UNFAIR ADVANTAGES FOR BILLIONAIRES

In addition to raising the floor, we need policies and rule changes that eliminate the unfair advantages that flow to billionaires and transnational corporations. Such policies could open opportunities for those historically excluded by race, gender, and location.

Reduce Money's Distorting Influence in Politics

As discussed earlier, the ultimate solution to billionaire power is policies that prevent antidemocratic concentrations of wealth. At the same time, we need to institute campaign finance reforms—including public financing of elections, elimination of super PACs, banning corporate contributions and influence, and timely disclosure of all political donations. Corporations should be prohibited from any participation in our democratic systems, including elections and bankrolling candidates, political parties, party conventions, and advertising aimed at influencing the outcome of elections and legislation.[9]

Revise Free Trade and Implement Fair Trade Rules

Most international "free trade" treaties benefit wealthy asset owners and shareholders while driving down workers' wages. Free trade agreements—typically negotiated on behalf of transnational companies—often pit nations and workers against one another in a race to lower the standards overseeing child labor laws and environmental protections, workers' rights to organize, and business regulation. Corporations operating in countries with the weakest standards are the biggest winners in this system. As an alternative, fair trade rules should elevate environmental and labor standards, so companies compete on the basis of other efficiencies.

Shut Down Global Tax Loopholes

Local jurisdictions attempting to levy taxes and invest in new economy institutions are undermined by global tax-avoidance practices. Individuals and corporations can shift trillions to offshore havens to escape taxation, accountability, and publicity. The United States itself operates as an "offshore" tax haven for international wealth. Low-bar corporate disclosure and reporting requirements in such states as Wyoming and Delaware make them ideal for banking illegal funds and hiding wealth.[10] The first step in shutting down global wealth hiding is to establish transparency reforms, such as disclosure of "beneficial ownership" of trusts, shell corporations, and anonymous entities.

DECONCENTRATING BILLIONAIRE WEALTH

Because of political capture by the billionaire class, it will be difficult to institute policies that raise the floor and reduce unfair advantages for billionaires, unless we directly tackle the concentration of wealth and power. While we might institute policies that discourage the wealthy from influencing the political system at the margins, the only way to ultimately protect the democratic system is to break up aggregations of power that flow from massive wealth. To deconcentrate billionaire wealth and power requires the restoration of progressive income and wealth taxes, antitrust laws, and reining in runaway CEO pay.

Restore Progressive Income Taxes

We should reinstate high taxes in the range of 50 to 70 percent for the highest-income groups, starting with steeply progressive taxes on the incomes of centi-millionaires and billionaires.

Eliminate Tax Preference for Income from Wealth

Our current tax code gives preferential treatment to income derived from wealth over income earned from work, by taxing capital gains at absurdly lower rates than wage income. One solution is to treat all wealth the same, no matter its provenance, while maintaining a progressive rate structure. Elders with low retirement income from investments will pay at lower rates, but billionaires reaping most of their income from capital will pay at higher rates.

Protect and Expand Inheritance Taxation

Established in 1916 as a response to the excesses of the Gilded Age, the estate tax is the only U.S. levy exclusively on the in-

"I would happily pay more in taxes, if somebody made me."

herited wealth of multimillionaires and billionaires. For decades, the estate tax helped deconcentrate income and wealth and even encouraged Gilded Age barons to turn over their fortunes and mansions to civic groups and charities.[11] In the 1920s, the then Treasury secretary cut estate tax rates. Over the last three decades, this inheritance tax has been cut to a point of near irrelevance, but it should be strengthened in the face of growing economic inequality. A robust estate or inheritance tax would discourage dynastic accumulations of wealth.

Levy a Wealth Tax on Billionaires

A progressive "net worth tax" on individual or household wealth over $50 million—including real estate, cash, investment funds, savings in insurance and pension plans, and personal trusts—would generate substantial revenue. But more important, if strong enough it could help reverse the accretion of billionaire power.

Create a Tax on Global Wealth

Given the mobility of capital in the digital age, nation-states should levy a coordinated global wealth tax in each country. A proposal to levy a 2 percent global minimum wealth tax has been advanced by groups like the Patriotic Millionaires, with funds flowing to individual nation-states. The G20 countries have begun conversations about the need for coordinated billionaire wealth taxes to protect democratic institutions.[12]

Strengthen Antitrust Laws

We have witnessed an extraordinary concentration of billionaire-backed corporate power over the past thirty-five years in almost every major sector—telecommunications, transportation, media, manufacturing, agriculture, extractive industries, and retail. Concentrating corporate power through monopolistic behavior—buying competitor companies and creating mega "parent" companies—threatens consumers, producers, and localities.[13] It also increases the wealth of billionaires by several fold. We need to enforce antitrust laws more boldly and consistently reduce such monopolies.[14] The Biden administration's Federal Trade Commission brought several antitrust actions against major corporations. After the reelection of Donald Trump, David Dayen writes, "State attorney generals are going to have to step up in the face of a pullback of enforcement at all levels of the federal government."[15]

Rein in CEO Pay and Corporate Incentive Systems

The CEO pay system is one cause of unequal wages and short-term corporate decision-making horizons. Action steps include linking a company's tax rate to the size of the gap between CEO and median worker pay, with a lower rate for companies with smaller ratios.[16]

Deconcentrating wealth has the twin positive benefits of diminishing billionaire wealth and diminishing poverty. Taxing extreme wealth generates revenue to make investments to offset the many harms caused by billionaire wealth extraction. Public opinion is aligned with fixing the areas "burned by billionaires" that have been discussed in this book. According to a 2024 Harris Poll, Americans think if billionaires were taxed at higher levels, those monies should be invested to improve affordable health care (58 percent), affordable housing (53 percent), food security (32 percent), improved infrastructure (29 percent), mental health services (28 percent), and climate mitigation (20 percent).[17]

REWIRING THE ECONOMY TO BLOCK BILLIONAIRE DISRUPTION

Rewiring the economy to prevent the creation of billionaires will reduce the excesses of extractive capitalism and consumption and promote broader income and wealth distribution.

Broaden Ownership

Worker ownership of enterprises helps to ensure that workers share the benefits of productivity gains and wealth creation. Broadly owned enterprises, which range from having employee shareholders to full worker ownership, build wealth and assets for workers and promote greater equality. Research indicates that such firms are not only better for workers but also more productive and stable than more traditional investor-owned companies.[18]

Rewire Finance

In our current finance system, voluminous personal debt held by the non-wealthy, and their interest payments, basically transfer wealth from the bottom of the wealth scale to the billionaire class, turning large sections of the financial sector into extractive enterprises rather than the stable lending systems needed for small business and healthy economic activity. Part of the solution is to strengthen and expand the grassroots financial sector that already includes more than 1,000 community development financial institutions, which across the United States includes 492 loan funds, 176 bank-holding companies, banks, or thrifts, 177 community development credit unions, and 13 community-oriented venture capital firms.[19] We can also create a network of state public banks and establish a national infrastructure bank. Taxing billionaire speculation through something like a Wall Street financial transaction tax could discourage reckless and hyper-extractive finance practices and generate $777 billion over ten years for public investments.[20]

Rewire the Corporation

Corporations should be rewired to serve broader interests beyond wealth creation for executives and shareholders. This includes reforms to broaden governance and ownership and legislate charters that disallow irresponsible behaviors. Transnational corporations should have federal charters requiring the governing board of a corporation to include all major stakeholders, including representation from consumers, employees, localities where the company operates, and environmental organizations. On the proactive side, we should encourage the formation of more "for benefit" or B corporations, for-profit entities recognized by the majority of U.S.

states that are driven by both mission and profit. This would help to establish a larger sector of "high-road" corporations that meet rigorous standards of social and environmental performance, accountability, and transparency.[21]

GAME-CHANGING CAMPAIGNS

In our current political arena, billionaires have kept many of these solutions off the national policy agenda through lobbying and campaign contributions that buy favor with key lawmakers. The average voter does not ordinarily tune in to these kinds of highly complex tax proposals as they are being debated, thinking that they have no implication for their own welfare. Therefore, it would be important to press for what I call "game-changing policy campaigns" that more clearly benefit and capture the interest of ordinary people. A "game-changing" policy campaign would ideally do three things:

* Reduce the concentration of billionaire wealth and power
* Open economic opportunities to those excluded in the current system
* Capture the imagination of a wide constituency of people willing to fight for it

Here are three examples of game-changing campaigns:

Fund Debt-Free Higher Education Through a Tax on Billionaire Inheritances

A tax on billionaire estates could fund an "education opportunity fund" for reducing or eliminating college student debt. Bill Gates Sr. advocated making college tuition grants to young people who complete two years of civilian or military service. Gates called this a "G.I. Bill for the next generation."[22] Imagine a political movement made up of the 44 million households that currently hold $1.4 trillion in student debt.[23]

Pay Dividends for the Use of Common Assets (or Pollution of the Commons)

The government could charge corporations for the use of common assets and pay out dividends to every resident on a one-person, one-share basis. For example, residents of Alaska receive annual dividends from the Alaska Permanent Fund, which shares the oil wealth on a per capita basis.[24] Conversely, the government could charge polluting companies and distribute the gains to people affected. For example, a "cap and dividend" system could cap the amount of carbon dumped in the atmosphere and charge polluters a dumping fee. The revenue would be paid out to energy consumers per capita, partly to offset higher energy costs.[25]

Tax Private Jet Pollution and Invest in Green Infrastructure

Increasing taxes on private jet fuel and applying the revenue to fund the transition to green infrastructure, like wind and solar energy, would help the economy become less dependent on fossil fuels and potentially reduce impacts from climate change.[26]

These are examples of pathways forward to "unrig" the rules of the economy that have been funneling wealth to the billionaire class. Implementing such rule changes would reverse the four-decade process of wealth concentration.

CONCLUSION

> *The world has enough for everyone's needs but not everyone's greed.*
>
> —Mahatma Gandhi

WITHOUT CONCERTED INTERVENTIONS TO DECONCENTRATE wealth and power, we are becoming an *oligarchy on autopilot.* Wealth extraction and accumulation, political capture, and billionaire growth are now a self-perpetuating cycle.

Without a course correction, within a decade we will see our first trillionaires and ever more of the nation's treasure flowing into the hands of a tiny sliver of the population. Today, 2,700 global billionaires hold more than $14 trillion (with 813 U.S. billionaires holding over $6.7 trillion). It's not inconceivable that by 2030, 5,000 global billionaires and trillionaires will hold and control $40 trillion, and a growing percentage of the global wealth pie.

On a parallel track, if we don't reverse course on climate change, the year 2030 will see even further ecological disruption as we skate past several ecological points of no return. These trends are connected, as discussed, as the billionaire class are the planet's super-emitters and drivers of investment in the fossil fuel industry. With climate change, we will literally be "burned by billionaires." The residents of Trillionaireville will probably by then be working to build mansions on other planets. The fictional dystopia of Elysium could very well come to pass.

Historians like Peter Turchin have forecasted what happens to societies with extreme inequality: a growing immiseration for the majority and dizzying concentrations of wealth for the few eventually foster social and political breakdown. Turchin draws this conclusion from well-known historical events like the French Revolution, the overthrow of the Russian czars, and the Cuban revolution—all popular uprisings to extreme levels of wealth in the hands of a few, and the corruption that accompanies it. In a contemporary U.S. context, in addition to the rising authoritarianism that we are already seeing, this could take many forms, including collapse of civil order and governance, political fragmentation, economic depression, and civil war. It's not a pretty picture. I suspect that's why he titled his book *End Times.*

In the aftermath of the 2024 presidential election, Turchin reflected on the deeper undercurrents and impersonal social forces that propelled Trump to victory. Turchin identified the three factors at work as "popular immiseration" (wage stagnation, declining well-being), "elite overproduction" (with wealth holders competing against one another), and "state breakdown" (stay tuned). Turchin believes Trump will be unable to address the underlying conditions that gave rise to his rebellion. We are heading into a "lasting age of discord," in Turchin's words.[1]

I don't want to offer a phony pep talk on the possibilities for change. But I do want to conclude with two things I know to be true and a few promising "signs of the times."

UNDERSTANDING THE HARMS OF CONCENTRATED WEALTH

One thing for certain is that the first step in shifting this trajectory is a greater understanding of the personal harms of concentrated wealth and power to each and every American. The false narratives that exalt billionaires—allowing them to grab more wealth and power—are a form of modern-day idolatry. The program outlined in the previous chapter includes many of the steps that other societies have undertaken to reverse extreme wealth inequality. But nothing will happen if we don't fully appreciate the fact that our lives and prosperity are being burned by billionaires.

A WORLD WITHOUT BILLIONAIRES

The second truth is that we need a positive vision of a world without billionaires. The best measure of economic success is not the number of billionaires in a society, but the reduction and elimination of poverty from it. A healthy society would have fewer billionaires, and along with it, fewer potholes, greater health, and more economically secure working- and middle-class households. Let us imagine a public sphere that is the opposite of disinvested, deteriorated, and neglected. There is enough, ample, plenty for all to have a decent life. To paraphrase Gandhi, there is enough for everyone's need, but not for anyone's greed.[2]

A healthy U.S. society would afford for all what many European countries have as the norm, but which in our country is often considered the privileges of Affluent Town: gleaming libraries and public schools with modern equipment, clean and accessible public transportation, affordable, well-designed housing, and pristine recreational facilities and public parks. We would be healthy, not because of high-tech hospitals, but because our bodies and minds are thriving with nutritious food, unpolluted environments, and social cohesion that recognizes that we are in a state of deep interconnection and that an injury to one is an injury to all.

Imagine private sufficiency alongside public luxury—and the feelings of security and well-being that would result in a more equitable, less economically precarious society. Envision the diminished stress and a contentment that comes from belonging and contributing.

NOTICE THE CRACKS IN THE SYSTEM

This book is chock-full of the alarming indicators of a society dominated by billionaires. But there are cracks in what sometimes appears to be an impermeable system of concentrated wealth and power. It is important to notice and share these with one another to keep our spirits up and an alternative vision alive.

Here are just a few signs of resistance that I see today:

* A growing movement to build social housing for all. Many communities have organizations working to build permanently affordable housing outside the speculative market—including community land trusts for housing, and mobile home resident cooperatives with people owning their own destiny.

* A renewed labor movement that is winning battles for higher wages and the right to collectively bargain. In the years since the pandemic, several unions—including those representing autoworkers, flight attendants, screenwriters, and actors—have successfully organized strikes (or threats to strike), winning significant pay and benefit raises in the process. Labor organizers have also made inroads in organizing unions in some Amazon plants. Leaders like Shawn Fain of the United Autoworkers are speaking out against billionaire greed and for the dignity of workers. A Gallup Poll found two-thirds of Americans consider themselves union supporters.[3]

* An environmental justice movement that is holding climate criminals to account and initiating litigation to help states recover their costs in addressing climate change–induced disasters.

* Growing public support for policies to rein in billionaires. Seventy-one percent of likely voters, including 53 percent of Republicans, think billionaires should pay more in taxes.[4] And 80 percent favor higher taxes on corporations with CEOs that make more than fifty times what their employees earn.[5]

* Growing disdain for the billionaire class among the younger generation. Young people are significantly less enamored of billionaires than are their boomer elders, and believe these titans are making it harder for them to achieve their dreams. (By contrast,

72 percent of boomers believe "billionaires are good for the economy.") Huge majorities of all generations believe billionaires should butt out of politics.[6]

In an earlier chapter, I observed that residents of Richistan and Affluent Town are mostly on the same team, but not 100 percent. There are dissenters from within the wealth-owning classes and the wealth defense industry that serve them. Here are a few of the cracks in the upper echelons of the wealth extraction machinery:

* Wealthy individuals and families, through networks such as the Patriotic Millionaires, are speaking out in favor of higher taxes on the wealthy, higher wages for workers, campaign finance reform, and improvements to the laws governing philanthropy.[7]

* A veteran wealth adviser started a new firm to help wealthy clients entirely rethink their relationship to wealth.[8] She is helping to spark a "progressive advisor's movement" among tax attorneys, accountants, wealth managers, and family office staffers, urging them to work for a higher purpose: aiding their clients to deploy wealth to *heal the harms caused by wealth extraction.*[9]

* A segment of these wealth managers, members of the trusted retinuef enablers that serve the ultra-wealthy, are defecting, blowing the whistle on systemic abuses and helping craft laws to close the tax loopholes that they helped to create. Marlena Sonn, an adviser to

members of the Getty family, was fired for urging family members to pay their California taxes and went public to reveal the behavior.[10]

* Wealth holders are rethinking "how much is enough" and pledging to radically redistribute their wealth, seeking ways to share decision-making and power to "decolonize wealth."[11]

These people are by no means a majority of the extremely wealthy, but they are positive indicators that not everyone supports the billionaire wealth extraction program.

BECOME A CRACK IN THE WEALTH EXTRACTION SYSTEM

My invitation to you is to consider ways that you can personally slow and thwart the wealth extraction system. Where there is a crack, insert your toe and then your foot. Join in some of the social movements working to build a fair economy (see Inequality.org as a place to start). Here are a few good first steps:

* **Strengthen face-to-face community**. Get to know your neighbors better and practice neighborliness. Participate in coffee klatches and community meals. Foster interdependence and mutual aid, small steps toward a practice of solidarity.

* **Shift to billionaire-free media and social media**. Get your information from sources that are not

owned and controlled by billionaires. There are plenty out there, but they are under assault and need our eyes, ears, and contributions.[12]

* **Participate where you have agency**. We're going to need all hands on deck to maintain an independent civil society. Participate in local government—as well as supporting candidates and leaders who are independent of the billionaire agenda, who will work to advance some of the policies articulated in chapter 10. Voting is only a small fraction of the work we must do. Our society needs a higher level of engagement.

Let's take billionaire burn personally. Resolve to be a small crack in the wealth extraction system and work for a more balanced and healthy future.

ACKNOWLEDGMENTS

THIS BOOK IS DEDICATED TO MY COLLEAGUE SAM PIZZIgati, who since 1994 has been an important mentor and public scholar on matters of extreme inequality of wealth. Sam wrote the unparalleled book, *Greed and Good: Understanding and Overcoming the Inequality That Limits Our Lives*. Everything we've written since then is a coda to this foundational set of insights about the harms of inequality to us personally and societally. (The book can be downloaded for free at inequality.org/resources/books/greed-and-good).

Sam has been the dean and village elder to a community of activists, organizers, and scholars who have worked for decades to put these issues of inequality on the public agenda. A critical mass of this community has been based in (or passed through) the Institute for Policy Studies and the Program on Inequality and the Common Good (www.inequality.org).

Thanks for the support of IPS's leadership, including Tope Folarin, Kathleen Gaspard, LaShawn Walker, and John Cavanagh, who have fostered a collegial community of public scholars and campaigners. Our inequality team, including Sarah Anderson, Omar Ocampo, Reyanna James, Chris Mills Rodrigo, Bob Lord, Dedrick Asante-Muhammad, and Sam Pizzigati, think and write every day how billionaires are burning our commonwealth. I also delight every day in working with our IPS Charity Reform Project team, including Bella DeVaan, Helen Flannery, Dan Petegorsky, and Scott Ellis.

Some of these chapters build on research and reports we have done together, including the work on private jets, housing, billionaire impacts, and the racial wealth divide. For this, I'm thankful to Omar Ocampo, Kalena Thomhave, Bella Devaan, Helen Flannery, Dedrick Asante-Muhammad, and other colleagues for their work on this research. Also thanks to health researcher Stephen Bezruchka, Asher Miller and Richard Heinberg at Post Carbon Institute, Amy Chew at Popular Democracy, Kati Winchell at Stop Private Jet Expansion, and other collaborators in this field.

Part of this village extends to the staff and board of the Patriotic Millionaires, including fearless leader Erica Payne, who took time to brainstorm with me about the messaging of this book. Thanks to Alan Davis for sparking the conversations about "excessive wealth" and for your continuing faith in our work. Thanks to my own community of collaborators, including Josh Hoxie, Lissa Weinmann, Susan Healy, Peter Gould, Linda Farthing, Michael Gast, Stephen Prince, and Morris Pearl, who are always game to talk about the impact of billionaires.

Many thanks to the terrific team at The New Press, starting with the spark and leadership of Diane Wachtell, who proposed this book. Tanya Coke was a smart and thoughtful editor, bringing an intimacy to the book and making it infinitely better. Many thanks to the others on the New Press team, including Gia Gonzales, Maury Botton, Rachel Vega-DeCesario, and Nia Abrams. Thanks also to Carrie Hamilton for the cover design and Brian Mulligan for the book design.

I had several very helpful readers of early editions of the book. Many thanks to Gabriela Sandoval, director of the Excessive Wealth Disorder Institute for your careful review of this manuscript. Gratitude to Kalena Thomhave and Marcia Peters for thoughtful edits and suggestions. Thanks to Kalena for helping work out the data for Richistan.

Thanks to my bonus son, Sam Hannon, for a conversation about housing and billionaire disruption that motivated me to write a popular book. Thanks to my longtime friend Kay O'Rourke for her insights into pets.

Thanks to my family and the life we have created at the Springs Farm in Vermont and around New England, starting with my spouse, Mary Wallace Collins, the life of the party. Additional local thanks to Alex Lach, Ed Corpus, Emily Wagner, Luke Concannon, Stephanie Hollenberg, and the Guilford Coffee Klatch. Nora Collins is always a thoughtful sounding board and insightful editor. Thanks to Sam Hannon, Janelle Gordon, Morgan Harper Hannon, and Caleb Hannon, Cal Glover-Wessell, and the extended clan of cousins, aunties, and uncles that are the spice of life.

NOTES

INTRODUCTION: TAKE IT PERSONALLY

1. Chuck Collins, "2024: The Year of the Billionaire," Common Dreams, January 4, 2025. All billionaire wealth data estimates come from Forbes's "Real Time Billionaire List," January 1, 2025. Forbes also does an annual snapshot of global billionaires. According to the April 2024 snapshot, there are 2,781 global billionaires worth $14.2 trillion; the United States has 813 billionaires worth a combined $5.7 trillion.
2. "Americans and Billionaires Survey," Harris Poll Thought Leadership Practice, wave 2, August 2024.
3. Chuck Collins, "Updates: Billionaire Wealth, U.S. Job Losses and Pandemic Profiteers," Inequality.org, November 21, 2022. Other billionaire wealth stats are from *Forbes,* December 31, 2024.
4. Andrew Stanton, "Net Worths of Donald Trump's Billionaire Appointments," *Newsweek,* December 2, 2024.
5. Will Kenton, "Regulatory Capture Definition with Examples," *Investopedia,* August 1, 2024. Based on the economy theory of George Stigler. See Susan Dudley and Jerry Brito, "Regulation: A Primer," Mercatus Center, George Mason University, 2012.
6. Peter Turchin, *End Times: Elites, Counter-Elites, and the Path of Political Disintegration* (New York: Penguin Press, 2023).

7. Carter C. Price and Kathryn A. Edwards, "Trends in Income from 1975 to 2018," RAND Corporation, September 2020, www.rand.org/pubs/working_papers/WRA516-1.html.
8. Nick Hanauer, "The Top 1% of Americans Have Taken $50 Trillion from the Bottom 90%—and That's Made the U.S. Less Secure," *Time*, September 14, 2020.
9. Peter Turchin, *End Times: Elites, Counter-Elites, and the Path of Political Disintegration* (New York: Penguin Press, 2023).

1. WHAT DO WE MEAN BY "THE WEALTHY"?

1. Farhad Manjoo, "Abolish Billionaires," *New York Times*, February 6, 2019.
2. Stewart's article was eventually published as a book: Matthew Stewart, *The 9.9 Percent: The New Aristocracy That Is Entrenching Inequality and Warping Our Culture* (New York: Simon & Schuster, 2021).
3. Matthew Stewart, "The Birth of the New American Aristocracy," *The Atlantic*, June 2018.
4. Richard Reeves, *Dream Hoarders: How the American Upper Middle Class Is Leaving Everyone Else in the Dust, Why That Is a Problem, and What We Can Do About It* (Washington, DC: Brookings, 2017).
5. Steve Brill, "How the Boomers Broke America," *Time*, May 17, 2018.
6. Stewart, "Birth of the New American Aristocracy."
7. Robert Frank, *Richistan: A Journey Through the American Wealth Boom and the Lives of the New Rich* (New York: Crown Publishers, 2007), pp. 6–12. See Frank's "Inside Wealth" newsletter at CNBC, www.cnbc.com/inside-wealth-newsletter-with-robert-frank.
8. Grant Suneson, "Here's the List of the Most Affluent Town in Every State in the U.S.," *USA Today*, May 12, 2019.
9. Richard Florida, *The New Urban Crisis* (New York: Basic Books, 2017).
10. Stewart, "Birth of the New American Aristocracy." Reeves, *Dream Hoarders*.

11. Open Secrets donor database on 2018 election giving, "Donor Demographics," Open Secrets, www.opensecrets.org/overview/donordemographics.php?cycle=2018&filter=A.
12. Benjamin I. Page and Martin Gilens, *Democracy in America? What Has Gone Wrong and What We Can Do About It* (Chicago: University of Chicago Press, 2020).
13. Wealth data comes from the Survey of Consumer Finances, "Changes in U.S. Family Finances from 2019 to 2022: Evidence from the Survey of Consumer Finances," Board of Governors of the Federal Reserve System, October 18, 2023, www.federalreserve.gov/econres/scfindex.htm?mod=article_inline.
14. Income data in this section comes from the U.S. Census Bureau, "Income in the United States: 2023," U.S. Census Bureau, September 10, 2024, Report P60-282, www.census.gov/library/publications/2024/demo/p60-282.html.
15. See Thomas J. Stanley and William D. Danko, *Millionaire Next Door: The Surprising Secrets of America's Wealthy* (New York: Pocket Books, 1996).
16. Distributional Financial Accounts, "Distribution of Household Wealth in the U.S. Since 1989," Board of Governors of the Federal Reserve System, first quarter 2024, www.federalreserve.gov/releases/z1/dataviz/dfa/index.html. Gabriel Zucman and Emmanuel Saez, "Wealth Inequality in the United States Since 1913," 2014, figures adapted to 2015 dollars, gabriel-zucman.eu/files/SaezZucman2014Slides.pdf. See updated 2016 data, eml.berkeley.edu/~saez/SaezZucman2016QJE.pdf.
17. These include so-called 501(c)(4) organizations. Learn more about dark money here, "Dark Money Secrets," Open Secrets, www.opensecrets.org/dark-money/basics, and here, "Dark Money Illuminated," Issue One, www.issueone.org/wp-content/uploads/2018/09/Dark-Money-Illuminated-Report.pdf.
18. Stewart, "Birth of the New American Aristocracy." Reeves, *Dream Hoarders*.
19. Frank, *Richistan*, p. 11.

20. Rob LaFranco, Grace Chung, and Chase Peterson-Withorn, "Forbes World's Billionaires List: The Richest in 2024," *Forbes,* April 2, 2024.
21. Michael Mechanic, "America's 806 Billionaires Are Now Richer Than Half the Population Combined—a Lot Richer," *Mother Jones,* April 11, 2024.
22. Chris Morris, "Elon Musk Could Become the World's First Trillionaire by 2027, Report Says," *Fortune,* September 9, 2024.

2. HOW DO PEOPLE BECOME BILLIONAIRES?

1. As inequality and precariousness grow, there are more insidious versions of these get-rich-quick schemes bordering on scams. See Bomikazi Zeta and Abdul Latif Alhassan, "Get-Rich-Quick Schemes, Pyramids and Ponzis: Five Signs You're Being Scammed," The Conversation, May 21, 2023.
2. The original quote from Balzac's *Le Pere Goriot* is *"Le secret des grandes fortunes sans cause apparente est un crime oublié, parce qu'il a été proprement fait"* (The secret of a great success for which you are at a loss to account is a crime that has never been found out, because it was properly executed). Honoré de Balzac, *Le Père Goriot* (Oxford Reference, 1835).
3. Chuck Collins, "Updates: Billionaire Wealth, U.S. Job Losses and Pandemic Profiteers," Inequality.org, November 21, 2022.
4. Jack Collison, "The Impact of Online Food Delivery Services on Restaurant Sales," Stanford University, Department of Economics, Spring 2020.
5. Scott Carpenter and Ivan Levingston, "Food Delivery Billionaires See Fortunes Swoon as Pandemic Ebbs," Bloomberg, June 7, 2022.
6. Carpenter and Levingston. To cinematically experience the life of a UK delivery driver and the risks these drivers take, see Ken Loach's film, *Sorry We Missed You,* and see my review, Chuck Collins, "A Film Recommendation: Sorry We Missed You," Inequality.org, April 13, 2020.

7. Food Processing, "Food Processing's Top 100—2024," *Food Processing*, 2024.
8. Tito Garcia was named Entrepreneur of the Year in 2023. The following year the company was fined by the U.S. Department of Labor for wage and hour violations. Bob Audette," Tito's Taqueria Fined by U.S. Labor Department for Wage Violations," *Brattleboro Reformer*, July 22, 2024.
9. Alexis Goldstein, "These Invisible Whales Could Sink the Economy," *New York Times*, May 18, 2021. Also see Chuck Collins, "How Billionaires' Secretive Speculation Threatens the Next Financial Meltdown," *MarketWatch*, June 8, 2021.
10. See my interview with Brooke Harrington, author of *Capital Without Borders*: "Agents of Inequality: How Wealth Managers to the Superrich Undermine Society and What We Can Do About It," *The Nation*, June 21, 2017.
11. Kalena Thomhave and Chuck Collins, "Dynasty Trusts: How the Wealthy Shield Trillions from Taxation Onshore," Institute for Policy Studies, June 2021.
12. Kalena Thomhave and Chuck Collins, "Billionaire Enabler States: How U.S. States Captured by the Trust Industry Help the World's Wealthy Hide Their Fortunes," Institute for Policy Studies, September 2022.
13. Thomhave and Collins, "Dynasty Trusts."
14. Jorja Seimons, "Supreme Court Curbs EPA Regulatory Power After Koch-Tied Groups Push," Open Secrets, July 25, 2022. See Jane Mayer, *Dark Money: The Hidden History of the Billionaires Behind the Rise of the Radical Right* (New York: Random House, 2016); Scott Bland, "George Soros' Quiet Overhaul of the U.S. Justice System," *Politico*, August 30, 2016.
15. Sam Pizzigati, "The Rich That Own the House Next Door," Inequality.org, January 5, 2024.
16. Peter Turchin, *End Times: Elites, Counter-Elites, and the Path of Political Disintegration* (New York: Penguin Press, 2023). Also see Turchin's website, peterturchin.com.

17. "Average Tax Rate in the United States in 2020, by Income Percentile," Statistica, www.statista.com/statistics/318079/average-tax-rate-in-the-us-by-income-percentile.
18. Greg Leiserson and Dany Yagan, "What Is the Average Federal Individual Income Tax Rate on the Wealthiest Americans?" Council of Economic Advisers, September 23, 2021.
19. Eileen Appelbaum and Rosemary Batt, "Private Equity Buyouts in Healthcare: Who Wins, Who Loses?" (Institute for New Economic Thinking, working paper 118, March 25, 2020).
20. Ludovic Phalippou, "An Inconvenient Fact: Private Equity Returns & the Billionaire Factory" (University of Oxford, Said Business School, working paper, June 10, 2020).
21. Turchin, *End Times*. Also see Turchin's website, peterturchin.com.
22. These words are from William Bernstein, "The Wealth Pump," *VettaFi*, August 7, 2023, www.advisorperspectives.com/articles/2023/08/07/global-markets-wealth-william-bernstein. He notes how the "wealth pump" is a nifty description of a phenomenon others have also described. For example, Mancur Olson describes something like a wealth pump in his 1982 survey, *The Rise and Decline of Nations* (New Haven: Yale University Press, 1982).

3. WHAT CREATED SO MANY BILLIONAIRES?

1. Chuck Collins, "801 Billionaires Hold a Combined $6.2 Trillion in Wealth," Inequality.org, September 17, 2024.
2. The average CEO-to-worker pay ratio was 268 to 1 for S&P 500 Index companies in 2023. "Executive Paywatch," AFL-CIO, 2023. https://aflcio.org/paywatch.
3. Kate Dore, "IRS Announces Bigger Estate and Gift Tax Exemption for 2025," CNBC, October 22, 2024.
4. "Share of Corporate Equities and Mutual Fund Shares Held by the Top 1%," Federal Reserve Bank of St. Louis, June 14, 2024, fred.stlouisfed.org/series/WFRBST01122.

5. Oliver Armantier, Luis Armona, Giacomo De Giorgi, and Wilbert van der Klaauw, "Which Households Have Negative Wealth?" New York Federal Reserve, August 1, 2016, libertystreeteconomics.newyorkfed.org/2016/08/which-households-have-negative-wealth.
6. Briana Sullivan, Donald Hays, and Neil Bennett, "Households with a White, Non-Hispanic Householder Were Ten Times Wealthier Than Those with a Black Householder in 2021," U.S. Census Bureau, April 23, 2024, www.census.gov/library/stories/2024/04/wealth-by-race.html-Sullivan, Hays, and Bennett.
7. Oliver P. Hauser and Michael I. Norton, "(Mis)perceptions of Inequality," *Current Opinion in Psychology* 18 (2017): 21–25.
8. The top tax rates came down steadily starting in 1961 under President John F. Kennedy. See Sam Pizzigati, "Reagan's Tax Reform Was a Bipartisan Effort of Surrender to America's Deepest Pockets," Institute for Policy Studies, May 5, 2017.
9. "The Productivity-Pay Gap," Economic Policy Institute, updated October 2022, www.epi.org/productivity-pay-gap.
10. Publicly traded firms contribute less to employment and GDP than they did in the 1970s. Frederik P. Schlingemann and Rene M. Stulz, "Has the Stock Market Become Less Representative of the Economy?" (NBER working paper 27943, October 2020), www.nber.org/system/files/working_papers/w27942/revisions/w27942.rev0.pdf.
11. "Total Market Value of U.S. Stock Market," Siblis Research, siblis-research.com/data/us-stock-market-value.
12. "Share of Corporate Equities."
13. Irina Ivanova, "The Running of the Bulls in 2023 Was More Like the Waddle of the Fat Cats," *Fortune,* January 13, 2024, fortune.com/2024/01/13/how-rich-wealthy-stock-market-investors-inequality-day-traders-record-high.
14. "Share of Corporate Equities."
15. "Share of Corporate Equities and Mutual Fund Shares Held by 90th to 99th Wealth Percentiles," Federal Reserve Bank of St. Louis, June 14, 2024, fred.stlouisfed.org/series/WFRBSN09149.

16. Lily Katz and Chen Zhao, "U.S. Housing Market Recovers the Nearly $3 Trillion It Lost, Hitting Record $47 Trillion in Total Value," Redfin, August 11, 2023.
17. Nick Stonnington, "How Democratization Is Paving a Path of Continued Growth in the Stock Market," *Forbes,* March 3, 2021.
18. Matt Phillips, "A Record Share of U.S. Households Now Own Stocks," *Axios,* October 18, 2023.
19. Gillian Tett, "The Magnificent Seven Is Not the Only Concentration America Should Worry About," *Financial Times,* January 4, 2024.
20. Mary Whitfill Roeloffs, "New Billionaires Inherited More Than They Earned Last Year, UBS Report Says," *Forbes,* November 30, 2023.
21. Daniel Neligh, Maria Clara Cobo, and Andre Tartar, "A $105 Trillion Inheritance Windfall Is on the Way for US Heirs," *Bloomberg,* December 5, 2024.

PART TWO: THE BILLIONAIRE BURN: HOW THE WEALTH OF A FEW IMPOVERISHES THE MANY

1. Will Hutton, "Log Cabin to White House? Not Anymore," *Observer of London,* April 28, 2002.

4. BILLIONAIRES ARE TRASHING THE PLANET

1. To learn more about the concept of planetary boundaries, see "Planetary Boundaries," Stockholm Resilience Centre, www.stockholmresilience.org/research/planetary-boundaries.html. On insect decline, see Oliver Millman, *The Insect Crisis: The Fall of the Tiny Empires That Run the World* (New York: W.W. Norton, 2022).
2. "Calculate Your Carbon Footprint," Nature Conservancy, 2024, www.nature.org.
3. "Climate Equality: A Planet for the 99%," Oxfam, November 2023.

4. "State of the Climate: 2024 Will Be First Year Above 1.5C of Warming," Carbon Brief, November 7, 2024.
5. "Climate Equality."
6. Larry Ellison's wealth estimate from *Forbes,* December 31, 2024. Beatriz Barros and Richard Wilk, "The Outsized Carbon Footprints of the Super-Rich," *Sustainability* 17 (2021).
7. Richard Wilk and Beatriz Barros, "Private Planes, Mansions, and Superyachts: What Gives Billionaires Like Musk and Abramovich Such a Massive Carbon Footprint," The Conversation, February 16, 2021.
8. Wilk and Barros.
9. "Real Time Billionaires," *Forbes,* www.forbes.com/profile/roman-abramovich/?sh=65f85d9a134a.
10. In the wake of the 2022 Russian invasion of Ukraine, Western governments sanctioned Abramovich, along with hundreds of other Russian oligarchs, freezing control of his yacht, London mansion, and $2.5 billion in assets from the sale of the Chelsea football team. See Mauricio Alencar, "Roman Abramovich and Ukraine: Where Is the Chelsea Sale Money Two Years On?" City A.M., May 30, 2024, www.cityam.com/abramovich-and-ukraine-where-is-the-chelsea-sale-money-two-years-on.
11. Wilk and Barros.
12. Katherine Kallergis, "Trust Tied to Gates Drops $21M on Wellington Horse Farm," *Real Deal,* July 2, 2019.
13. "Bill Gates Private Jet," SuperYachtFan, www.superyachtfan.com/yacht-owners/bill-gates/private-jet.
14. Meredith Woerner, "Neill Blomkamp's Elysium Is Real, and Located in Malibu," Gizmodo, September 11, 2013.
15. The web site, www.itsbetterupthere.com, no longer exists but you can read about it here: Alex Billington, "It's Better Up There—'Elysium' Viral Restarts with Citizenship Initiative," Firstshowing.net, July 12, 2012. https://www.firstshowing.net/2012/its-better-up-there-elysium-viral-restarts-with-citizenship-initiative/

16. "Climate Equality."
17. Doug Rushkoff, *Survival of the Richest: Escape Fantasies of the Tech Billionaires* (New York: W.W. Norton, 2022).
18. Chuck Collins and Emma de Goede, "Towering Excess: The Perils of the Luxury Real Estate Boom for Bostonians," Institute for Policy Studies, September 1, 2018.
19. "U.S. Environmental Footprint Factsheet," University of Michigan, Center for Sustainable Systems.
20. "Climate Equality."
21. "Spotlight on Private Jet Owners," Wealth-X, 2021, go.wealthx. com/2021-private-jet-owners.
22. Stefan Gossling, Andreas Humpe, and Jorge Cardoso Leitao, "Private Aviation Is Making a Growing Contribution to Climate Change," *Communications Earth and Environment* 5 (2024): 666.
23. Martin Guttridge-Hewitt, "Private Jet Spending Leaps Among Executives Despite Emissions Fears," *Environmental Journal*, January 24, 2024.
24. "Top 25 Global Flyers Failing to Reduce Business Travel Emissions," *Travel Smart*, March 28, 2023, travelsmartcampaign. org/library /top-25-global-flyers-failing-to-reduce-business-travel-emission.
25. Chuck Collins, Omar Ocampo, and Kalena Thomhave, "High Flyers 2023: How Ultra-Rich Private Jet Travel Costs the Rest of Us and Burns Up the Planet," Institute for Policy Studies, May 1, 2023. The Biden administration contends that the current rate is too low because private jets represent 7 percent of flights handled by the Federal Aviation Administration but contribute just 0.6 percent of the taxes in the fund. From Alan Rappeport, "Biden Targets Private Jets in Hunt for Tax Revenue," *New York Times*, March 21, 2024.
26. Chuck Collins, Omar Ocampo, Kalena Thomhave, and Jiaqin Wu, "Hanscom High Flyers: Private Jet Excess Doesn't Justify Airport Expansion," Institute for Policy Studies, October 2023.
27. Collins et al.

28. David Abel, "Billionaires Are Responsible for Large Amounts of Climate Pollution from Hanscom, a New Report Finds," *Boston Globe*, October 3, 2023.
29. "Greenwashing the Skies: How the Private Jet Lobby Uses Sustainable Aviation Fuels as a Marketing Ploy," Institute for Policy Studies, June 2024.
30. Comments by Francesca Webster, editor in chief, *Superyacht Times* on *BBC Business Daily*, "Building the Superyachts," November 7, 2024.
31. Ralph Dazert, "State of Yachting 2024," *Superyacht Times*, March 28, 2024 (presentation), www.youtube.com/watch?v=QKL1jhvCQC4. The full annual report, *The State of Yachting 2024*, is available at www.superyachttimes.com/yacht-news/the-state-of-yachting-2024.
32. Evan Osnos, "The Haves and Have Yachts," *New Yorker*, July 18, 2022.
33. "The Nebula Yacht Support Vessel: A Luxurious Companion for SuperYachts," SuperYachtFan, www.superyachtfan.com/yacht/nebula.
34. Sian Boyle, "Billionaires' Sail of the Century," *Daily Mail*, September 26, 2021. Also see: "About the Monaco Yacht Show," www.monacoyachtshow.com/en/about-the-mys.
35. Mark DeCambre, "Media Mogul David Geffen Observes a Sunset from His $400 Million Superyacht, as Coronavirus Ravages His Native New York: 'I'm Hoping Everybody Is Staying Safe,'" *Marketwatch*, March 30, 2020.
36. Osnos, "Haves and Have Yachts."
37. Beatriz Barros and Richard Wilk, "The Outsized Carbon Footprints of the Super-Rich," *Sustainability* 17 (2021).
38. There are 5,787 superyachts in the fleet as of spring 2024. Dazert, "State of Yachting 2024."
39. Joe Fassler, "The Superyachts of Billionaires Are Starting to Look a Lot Like Theft," *New York Times*, April 10, 2023.
40. "Carbon Billionaires: The Investment Emissions of the World's Richest People," Oxfam, 2022. The study assigns scope 1 and scope 2

emissions of the corporations these individuals invested in based on their equity stakes.

41. "Top 5 Ways Billionaires Are Driving Climate Change," *Climate Equality: A Planet for the 99%*, Oxfam, November 20, 2023.
42. More than nine thousand companies have joined the Race to Zero, pledging to take rigorous, immediate action to halve global emissions by 2030. See "For a Livable Climate: Net-Zero Commitments Must Be Backed by Credible Action," United Nations, www.un.org/en/climatechange/net-zero-coalition, and the Race to Zero pledge website, climatechampions.unfccc.int/system/race-to-zero. These include fifty oil and gas companies: Eklavya Gupte, Claudia Carpenter, Ivy Yin, and Jennifer Gnana, "COP28: Fifty Oil and Gas Companies Sign Net Zero, Methane Pledges," S&P Global, December 2, 2023, www.spglobal.com/commodityinsights/en/market-insights/latest-news/energy-transition/120223-cop28-fifty-oil-and-gas-companies-sign-net-zero-methane-pledges.
43. Neela Banerjee, John H. Cushman Jr., David Hasemyer, and Lisa Song, "Exxon: The Road Not Taken," *Inside Climate News*, 2015.
44. See "All Eyes on the Climate Criminals," www.climatecriminals.org.
45. Kelcy Warren is infamous for using litigation, so-called SLAPP suits—"strategic lawsuits against public participation"—to intimidate environmental activists.
46. *Banking on Climate Chaos: Fossil Fuel Finance Report 2024*, www.bankingonclimatechaos.org/?bank=JPMorgan%20Chase#full data-panel.
47. Dana Drugmand, "World's Biggest Banks Poured $673 Billion into Fossil Fuels Last Year," *DeSmog*, April 12, 2023. And see the report *Banking on Climate Chaos: Fossil Fuel Finance Report 2024*.
48. "Chase: Protect the Verde Island Passage," Rainforest Action Network, act.ran.org/page/52064/petition/1?locale=en-US. Also see the report *Banking on Climate Chaos: Fossil Fuel Finance Report 2024*.

49. Christopher Helman, "Fracking Pioneer Harold Hamm Explains How America Became the World's Energy Superpower," *Forbes,* July 31, 2023.
50. Josh Dawsey and Maxine Joselow, "This Oil Tycoon Brings in Millions for Trump, and May Set His Agenda," *Washington Post,* August 13, 2024.
51. Emma Garnett and Charlotte A. Kukowski, "Six Ways Inequality Holds Back Climate Action," The Conversation, January 15, 2024.
52. Joe Fassler, "The Superyachts of Billionaires Are Starting to Look a Lot Like Theft," *New York Times,* April 10, 2023.
53. Nicolas Baumard and Coralie Chevallier, "The Environmental Impact of Private Jets Is Largely Underestimated," *Le Monde,* September 13, 2022.
54. Richard Wilkinson and Kate Pickett, "Why the World Cannot Afford the Rich," Earth4All, March 20, 2024, earth4all.life/views/why-the-world-cannot-afford-the-rich.

5. BILLIONAIRES ARE MAKING YOU PAY HIGHER TAXES

1. In 2018 almost 17 percent of the benefits of the home mortgage interest deduction subsidy went to the top 1 percent of households, and 80 percent of the benefits went to households in the top 20 percent of the income distribution. Only 4 percent accrued to households in the middle-income quintile. William G. Gale, "Chipping Away at the Mortgage Deduction," Brookings Institution, May 13, 2019.
2. Chuck Collins, Omar Ocampo, and Kalena Thomhave, "High Flyers 2023: How Ultra-Rich Private Jet Travel Costs the Rest of Us and Burns Up the Planet," Institute for Policy Studies, May 1, 2023.
3. International Consortium of Investigative Journalists. On the Pandora Papers, see "An ICIJ Investigation: The Pandora Papers,"

www.icij.org/investigations/pandora-papers; on the Panama Papers, see "An ICIJ Investigation: The Panama Papers," www.icij.org/tags/panama-papers/overview.

4. Jesse Eisinger, Jeff Ernsthausen, and Paul Kiel, "The Secret IRS Files: Trove of Never-Before-Seen Records Reveal How the Wealthiest Avoid Income Tax," ProPublica, June 8, 2021.
5. See Eisinger, Ernsthausen, and Kiel, "Secret IRS Files"; and Paul Kiel, Jeff Ernsthausen, and Jesse Eisinger, "You May Be Paying a Higher Tax Rate Than a Billionaire," ProPublica, June 8, 2021.
6. Kate Dore, "IRS Announces Bigger Estate and Gift Tax Exemption for 2025," CNBC, October 22, 2024.
7. All fifty states had an estate tax prior to 2001, when the federal law changes phased out the way that states "piggybacked" on the federal law. States had to proactively enact state-level estate and inheritance taxes. Sixteen states and the District of Columbia did: Connecticut, Hawaii, Illinois, Iowa, Maine, Maryland, Massachusetts, Minnesota, Nebraska, New Jersey, New York, Oregon, Pennsylvania, Rhode Island, Washington, Vermont.
8. The 2017 provision allows chapter S corporations to pass on tax liabilities to individual shareholders to pay as individual income tax. For information about chapter S corporations, see "S Corporations," Internal Revenue Service, www.irs.gov/businesses/small-businesses-self-employed/s-corporations.
9. Daniel Shaviro, "Apparently Income Isn't Just Income Anymore," *Start Making Sense,* December 16, 2017, danshaviro.blogspot.com/2017/12/apparently-income-isnt-just-income-any.html.
10. Tobias Salinger, "Tax Planners See Uncertainty, Opportunity in Pass-Through Deduction," *Financial Planning,* May 25, 2018.
11. Robert Faturechi and Justin Elliot, "How the Trump Tax Law Created a Loophole That Lets Top Executives Net Millions by Slashing Their Own Salaries," ProPublica, April 19, 2021.
12. Patriotic Millionaires, *Crack the Code 2.0: Proposed Internal Revenue Code of 2026,* April 2024, taxtherich.com/the-plan.

13. Joel Friedman, "The Decline of Corporate Income Tax Revenues," Center on Budget and Policy Priorities, October 24, 2003.
14. "Historical Tables," table 2.1, "Receipts by Source: 1934–2028," and table 2.3, "Receipts by Source as Percentages of GDP: 1934–2028," Office of Management and Budget, 2003. Also see "Briefing Book," Tax Policy Center, January 2024.
15. Matt Gardner, Michael Ettlinger, Spandan Marasini, and Steve Wamhoff, "Corporate Taxes Before and After the Trump Tax Law," Institute on Taxation and Economic Policy, May 2024.
16. Chuck Marr, "Record Stock Buybacks Bolster Case for Raising Corporate Tax Rate," Center on Budget and Policy Priorities, June 24, 2024.
17. Cortney Sanders and Michael Leachman, "Step One to an Antiracist State Revenue Policy: Eliminate Criminal Justice Fees and Reform Fines," Center on Budget and Policy Priorities, September 17, 2021.
18. Lisa Riordan Seville, "Black St. Louis Suburbs Hit with Ticket Blitz," *NBC News*, August 22, 2014.
19. Chuck Collins, Josh Hoxie, and Jessicah Pierre, "Restoring Opportunity: Taxing Wealth to Fund College for All in California," Institute for Policy Studies, May 2018.
20. Donna Fuscaldo, "13 States That Tax Groceries," American Association of Retired Persons, February 2, 2024, www.aarp.org/money/taxes/info-2024/states-that-tax-groceries.html.
21. Jackson Brainerd, "What Happens When States Ditch Income Tax for Sales Tax?" National Conference of State Legislatures, February 14, 2024.
22. Institute on Taxation and Economic Policy, *Who Pays? A Distributional Analysis of the Tax Systems in All 50 States,* January 2024, itep.org/whopays-7th-edition.
23. See Chuck Collins, *The Wealth Hoarders: How Billionaires Pay Millions to Hide Trillions* (Cambridge: Polity Books, 2021), www.wealthhoarders.com.

24. See Collins, *Wealth Hoarders,* chap. "All in the Family Office." Also see Ben Stupples, "How New Wealth, Few Rules, Fuel Family Office Boom," Bloomberg, September 1, 2023.
25. James S. Henry, "Taxing Tax Havens," *Foreign Affairs,* April 12, 2016. Also see Collins, *Wealth Hoarders* Kalena Thomhave and Chuck Collins, "Billionaire Enabler States: How U.S. States Captured by the Trust Industry Help the World's Wealthy Hide Their Fortunes," Institute for Policy Studies, September 2022.
26. "15 Billionaires Top New List of America's Rich," Associated Press, September 28, 1983 (archive, Newspapers.com).
27. Phoebe Liu and Matt Durot, "Elon Musk Is Now Worth More Than $400 Billion, the First Person to Cross That Mark," *Forbes,* December 11, 2024. As of December 31, 2024, Musk was worth over $425 billion, according to *Forbes.*
28. Chuck Collins, Joe Fitzgerald, Helen Flannery, Omar Ocampo, Sophia Paslaski, and Kalena Thomhave, "Silver Spoon Oligarchs: How America's 50 Largest Inherited-Wealth Dynasties Accelerate Inequality," Institute for Policy Studies, 2021.
29. The other motivation for lawmakers to pass the estate tax was to raise revenue to pay for World War I. See Bill Gates Sr. and Chuck Collins, *Wealth and Our Commonwealth* (Boston: Beacon Press, 2003).
30. Bob Lord, "This Year's Real Halloween Horror," Inequality.org, October 25, 2017.
31. Jeff Ernsthausen, James Bandler, Justin Elliott, and Patricia Callahan, "More Than Half of America's 100 Richest People Exploit Special Trusts to Avoid Estate Taxes," ProPublica, September 28, 2021.
32. Zach Mider, "Accidental Tax Break Saves Wealthiest Americans $100 Billion," *Seattle Times,* February 15, 2014.
33. Theodore Schliefer, "Miriam Adelson Goes Searching for More Trump Donors," *New York Times,* October 24, 2024.
34. Naomi Klein, "Donald Trump, Brett Kavanaugh, and the Rule of Pampered Princelings," The Intercept, October 10, 2018.

6. BILLIONAIRES ARE WRECKING THE HOUSING MARKET

1. "The 2023 Annual Homelessness Assessment Report (AHAR) to Congress," U.S. Department of Housing.
2. Jason DeParle, "Migrants and End of Covid Restrictions Fuel Jump in Homelessness," *New York Times*, December 27, 2024.
3. "America's Rental Housing 2024," Joint Center for Housing at Harvard University, www.jchs.harvard.edu/sites/default/files/reports/files/Harvard_JCHS_Americas_Rental_Housing_2024. pdf. Also see Annie Nova, "15 Million Renters Pay More for Housing Than They Can Afford. Here's How to Figure Out If You're One of Them," CNBC, February 19, 2023.
4. Alexander Hermann and Peyton Whitney, "Home Price-to-Income Ratio Reaches Record High," Joint Center for Housing Studies at Harvard University, January 22, 2024; Laya Neelakandan, "2023 Was the Least Affordable Homebuying Year in at Least 11 Years, Redfin Says," CNBC, December 7, 2023.
5. Katherine Clarke, *Billionaires' Row: Tycoons, High Rollers, and the Epic Race to Build the World's Most Exclusive Skyscrapers* (New York: Currency, 2023).
6. Esthefany Castillo, "The 'Airbnb Effect' on an Already High-Cost, Shrinking Housing Market," *Travel Noire*, August 3, 2022; Zhenpeng Zou, "Examining the Impact of Short-Term Rentals on Housing Prices in Washington, DC: Implications for Housing Policy and Equity," *Housing Policy Debate* 30, no. 2 (December 2019): 269–90; Kyle Barron, Edward Kung, and Davide Proserpio, "The Effect of Home-Sharing on House Prices and Rents: Evidence from Airbnb," March 2020, ssrn.com/abstract=3006832.
7. Sean O'Neill, "Short-Term Rentals Attract Private Equity Seeking New Asset Class," *Skift*, March 15, 2022. See also: Kevin Vandenboss, "Is Jeff Bezos Your Landlord? If He's Not Yet, He May Be Soon," Yahoo Finance, August 17, 2023.
8. Carlos Waters, "Wall Street Has Purchased Hundreds of Thousands of Single-Family Homes Since the Great Recession.

Here's What That Means for Rental Prices," CNBC, February 21, 2023.

9. Chuck Collins, "Taking on a Billionaire Landlord in the Twin Cities," *Yes!* March 17, 2021.
10. *Homes for Profit: Speculation and Investment in Greater Boston,* Metropolitan Area Planning Council, November 2023, homesforprofit.mapc.org/executive-summary.
11. Ronda Kaysen, "New Legislation Proposes to Take Wall Street Out of the Housing Market," *New York Times,* December 6, 2023.
12. Sheelah Kolhatkar, "What Happens When Investment Firms Acquire Trailer Parks," *New Yorker,* March 8, 2021.
13. Frank Rolfe, "The Truth About My Notorious Waffle House Quote," Mobile Home University, www.mobilehomeuniversity.com/articles/the-truth-about-my-notorious-waffle-house-quote.
14. "We manage $382 billion in assets, spanning 3 business segments and 600 investment vehicles, investing wisely and responsibly over the long-term." From "Our Business Segments," Carlyle Group, 2024, www.carlyle.com/#our-firm/1.
15. Gillian Tan, "Blackstone to Boost Mobile-Home Bet with $550 Million Deal," Bloomberg, September 14, 2020.
16. Kolhatkar, "What Happens."
17. Amanda Gokee, "'Mini Democracies' and Affordable N.H. Home Ownership," *Boston Globe,* November 30, 2023.
18. Chuck Collins and Emma de Goede, "Towering Excess: The Perils of the Luxury Real Estate Boom for Bostonians," Institute for Policy Studies, September 1, 2018; Claudiu Tiganescu, "JV Lands $153M for Affordable Project in Boston," *Multi-Housing News,* November 11, 2024.
19. Chuck Collins, *The Wealth Hoarders: How Billionaires Pay Millions to Hide Trillions* (Cambridge: Polity Books, 2021); also see www.wealthhoarders.com; Jeffrey A. Winters, "Wealth Defense and the Limits of Liberal Democracy" (paper presented at the APSA 2014 Annual Meeting), 40–43, papers.ssrn.com/sol3/papers.cfm?abstract_id=2452419.

20. Alexander Ferrer, Terra Graziani, Jacob Woocher, and Zachary Frederick, *The Vacancy Report: How Los Angeles Leaves Homes Empty and People Unhoused,* Strategic Alternatives for a Just Economy; Alliance of Californians for Community Empowerment; UCLA School of Law Community Economic Development Clinic, September 2020.
21. Louise Story and Stephanie Saul, "Stream of Foreign Wealth Flows to Elite New York Real Estate," *New York Times,* February 7, 2015.
22. Victoria Baranetsky, "You Should Have the Right to Know Your Landlord's Name," *Los Angeles Times,* February 24, 2021; see "Rental Housing Finance Survey," U.S. Census, www.census.gov/data-tools/demo/rhfs/#/?s_byGroup1=6.
23. Devon Pendleton, "Chinese Billionaire Is Second-Biggest Foreign Owner of US Land," Bloomberg, January 8, 2024, www.bloomberg.com/news/articles/2024-01-08/chinese-billionaire-named-as-one-of-america-s-biggest-landowners?srnd=premium-asia.
24. Gates on Reddit, as reported at Land Report, landreport.com/land-report-100/bill-gates.
25. Bass family. From Land Report: The four great-nephews of legendary wildcatter Sid Richardson (1891–1959) share ownership of their great-uncle's 32,000-acre San Jose Island off the Texas coast near Port Aransas. Ed Bass and his wife, Sasha, are currently revitalizing Sundance Square, a thirty-five-block entertainment district in downtown Fort Worth that they assumed full ownership of from his brothers in 2019. The jewel in the crown of downtown Fort Worth hosts 10 million visitors a year.
26. Pendleton, "Chinese Billionaire."

7. BILLIONAIRES ARE SUPERCHARGING THE RACIAL ECONOMIC DIVIDE

1. Dedrick Asante-Muhammad and Chuck Collins, "Still a Dream: Over 500 Years to Black Economic Equality," Institute for Policy Studies, August 2023.

2. Isabela Espadas Barros Leal, "A $1 Million Wealth Gap Now Divides White Families from Black and Hispanic Ones, Research Shows," *NBC News,* April 25, 2024.
3. Espadas Barros Leal.
4. Espadas Barros Leal.
5. Sakshi Venkatraman, "Asian Americans Have the Biggest Wealth Gap," *NBC News,* December 22, 2021.
6. Oliver Armantier, Luis Armona, Giacomo De Giorgi, and Wilbert van der Klaauw, "Which Households Have Negative Wealth?" New York Federal Reserve, August 1, 2016.
7. Briana Sullivan, Donald Hays, and Neil Bennett, "Households with a White, Non-Hispanic Householder Were Ten Times Wealthier Than Those with a Black Householder in 2021," U.S. Census Bureau, April 23, 2024, www.census.gov/library/stories/2024/04/wealth-by-race.html.
8. Rupert Neate, "Next Generation of Billionaires Collect More Wealth from Inheritance Than Work, Says UBS," *The Guardian,* November 30, 2023.

8. BILLIONAIRES ARE BAD FOR YOUR HEALTH

1. Richard Wilkinson and Kate Pickett, *The Spirit Level: Why Greater Equality Makes Societies Stronger* (London: Bloomsbury Press, 2009). Also see "Social Determinants of Health Literature Summaries," Healthy People 2030, U.S. Department of Health and Human Services, odphp.health.gov/healthypeople/priority-areas/social-determinants-health/literature-summaries.
2. Apoorva Rama, "National Health Expenditures, 2022: A Return to Pre-Pandemic Growth Rates as Spending on Physician Services Decelerates," American Medical Association, April 2024.
3. Emma Wager, Matthew McGough, Shameek Rakshit, Krutika Amin, and Cynthia Cox, "How Does Health Spending in the U.S. Compare

to Other Countries?" Peterson-KFF Health System Tracker, January 23, 2024, www.healthsystemtracker.org/chart-collection/health-spending-u-s-compare-countries.

4. OECD, *Health at a Glance 2023: OECD Indicators* (Paris: OECD Publishing, 2003), doi.org/10.1787/7a7afb35-en.
5. Stephen Bezruchka, *Inequality Kills Us All: Covid-19's Health Lessons for the World* (London: Routledge, 2023), 22.
6. Bezruchka, 39.
7. Penn Nursing, "History of Hospitals," University of Pennsylvania, www.nursing.upenn.edu/nhhc/nurses-institutions-caring/history-of-hospitals.
8. Eileen Appelbaum and Rosemary Batt, "Private Equity Buyouts in Healthcare: Who Wins, Who Loses?" (Institute for New Economic Thinking, working paper 118, March 25, 2020).
9. Gretchen Morgenson and Joshua Rosner, *These Are the Plunderers: How Private Equity Runs—and Wrecks—America* (New York: Simon & Schuster, 2023), 176–77.
10. Morgenson and Rosner, 196.
11. Morgenson and Rosner, 176, 196.
12. Hanna Krueger, Jessica Bartlett, and Brendan McCarthy, "Inside the Secret Financial Dealings of Steward CEO Ralph de la Torre," *Boston Globe*, September 3, 2024.
13. Robert Kuttner, "Reversing Private Equity's Looting of Hospitals," *American Prospect*, February 13, 2024.
14. Maureen Tkacik, "Massachusetts Wakes Up to a Hospital Nightmare," *American Prospect*, January 26, 2024.
15. Robert Weisman, "Bankruptcy Filings Cast Doubt on Optum Buyout of Steward's Physician's Network," *Boston Globe*, May 28, 2024.
16. "Evaluating Trends in Private Equity Ownership and Impacts on Health Outcomes, Costs, and Quality: Systematic Review," *BMJ* (2023), www.bmj.com/content/382/bmj-2023-075244. Also see Bethany McLean, "Senate Report: How Private Equity 'Gutted' Dozens of U.S. Hospitals," *Washington Post*, October 17, 2024.

17. McLean, "Senate Report."
18. Jennifer Tolbert, Rakesh Singh, and Patrick Drake, "The Uninsured Population and Health Coverage," KFF, May 28, 2024.
19. D. Cutler and G. Miller, "The Role of Public Health Improvements in Health Advances: The Twentieth-Century United States," *Demography* 42, no. 1 (2005): 1–22.
20. Richard G. Wilkinson and Kate E. Pickett, "Why the World Cannot Afford the Rich," *Nature* 627 (March 14, 2024), www.nature.com/articles/d41586-024-00723-3.
21. Anne Case and Angus Deaton, "United States of Despair," *Project Syndicate,* June 15, 2020, www.project-syndicate.org/commentary/deaths-of-despair-covid19-american-inequality-by-anne-case-and-angus-deaton-2020-06.
22. Angus Deaton and Lyndsey Jefferson, "Amidst America's Changing Politics, Deaths of Despair Persist," Chatham House, March 31, 2021.
23. Dawn Foster, "Kate Pickett and Richard Wilkinson: Inequality Strikes at Our Health and Happiness," *The Guardian,* September 18, 2018.
24. Benjamin Mueller and Eleanor Lutz, "U.S. Has Far Higher Covid Death Rate Than Other Wealthy Countries," *New York Times,* February 1, 2022.
25. Alisha Haridasani Gupta, "How 'Weathering' Contributes to Racial Health Disparities," *New York Times,* April 12, 2023. See the research of Dr. Arline Geronimus, "The Effects of Race, Residence, and Prenatal Care on the Relationship of Maternal Age to Neonatal Mortality," *American Journal of Public Health* 76, no 12 (1986): 1416–21, doi.org/10.2105/ajph.76.12.1416.
26. Alain de Botton, *Status Anxiety* (New York: Pantheon, 2004).
27. Bezruchka, *Inequality Kills Us All,* 54–55.
28. Brendan O'Shannassy, *Superyacht Captain: Life and Leadership in the World's Most Incredible Industry* (London: Adlard Coles, 2022), chap. "Saint-Tropez Sunset."

29. Stephen Bezruchka, interview with the author, June 5, 2024.
30. Anna Aizer, Adriana Lleras-Muney, and Katherine Michelmore, "The Effects of the 2021 Child Tax Credit on Child Developmental Outcomes" (National Bureau of Economic Research, working paper 32609, June 2024).
31. Richard Wilkinson, *Unhealthy Societies: The Afflictions of Inequality* (London: Routledge, 1997), 4.

9. BILLIONAIRES ARE STEALING YOUR VOTE AND VOICE

1. Jake Johnson, "UAW President Calls for Working Class Unity Against Billionaire 'Lap Dog' Donald Trump," *Common Dreams,* October 30, 2024.
2. Ezra Klein, "The Doom Loop of Oligarchy," *Vox,* April 11, 2014.
3. Trisha Thadani and Clara Ence Morse, "Elon Musk Is Now America's Largest Political Donor," *Washington Post,* December 6, 2024.
4. Robert Reich, "Timothy Mellon and the Political Peril of Dynastic Wealth," WhoWhatWhy Media, February 29, 2024.
5. See #34 ranking in "America's Richest Families," *Forbes,* September 12, 2024.
6. Reich, "Timothy Mellon."
7. D. Krcmaric, S.C. Nelson, and A. Roberts, "Billionaire Politicians: A Global Perspective," *Perspectives on Politics* 22, no. 2 (2024): 357–71.
8. Stephanie Kulke, "11% of the World's Billionaires Have Held or Sought Political Office," *Northeastern News,* October 27, 2023.
9. Karl Ever-Hillstrom, "Majority of Lawmakers in 116th Congress Are Millionaires," Open Secrets, April 23, 2020.
10. Dan Balz, "The Mega Rich Are the New Political Bosses. Is That Bad for Democracy?" *Washington Post,* December 2, 2023.
11. Robert S. Chirinko and Daniel J. Wilson, "Can Lower Tax Rates Be Bought? Business Rent-Seeking and Tax Competition Among U.S. States," *National Tax Journal* 63, no. 4, pt. 2 (2010): 967–94.

12. "Analysis: Koch Brothers Could Get Up to $1.4 Billion Tax Cut from Law They Helped Pass," Americans for Tax Fairness, January 24, 2018, americansfortaxfairness.org/koch-brothers-1-billion-tax-cut.
13. One of the early legal scholars to work on this was Jamie Raskin, now a member of Congress. Jamie Raskin and John Bonifaz, "Equal Protection and the Wealth Primary," *Yale Law & Policy Review* 11, no. 2 (1993): 273–332, www.jstor.org/stable/40239404.
14. Laura Doan, "Doug Burgum Is Giving $20 Gift Cards in Exchange for Campaign Donations. Experts Split on Whether That's Legal," *CBS News*, July 19, 2023.
15. Balz, "The Mega Rich."
16. "Billionaire Clans Spend Nearly $2 BILLION on 2024 Elections," Americans for Tax Fairness, October 29, 2024, americansfortaxfairness.org/billionaire-clans-spend-nearly-2-billion-2024-elections.
17. "Billionaire Clans Spend Nearly $2 BILLION."
18. Don McCanne, Comment on "Gilens and Page: Average Citizens Have Little Impact on Public Policy. Testing Theories of American Politics: Elites, Interest Groups, and Average Citizens," Physicians for National Health Policy, April 9, 2014.
19. Institute for Policy Research, "Democracy in America: Benjamin Page Argues Ordinary Citizens Are Not Being Represented," Northwestern University, February 19, 2018.
20. Jared Bernstein, "'Democracy in America?' An Interview with Authors Ben Page and Martin Gilens," *Washington Post*, January 23, 2018.
21. "Tracking 2024 Election Contributions and Spending," USA Facts, updated August 2, 2024.
22. "Tracking 2024 Election Contributions and Spending."
23. Anna Massoglia, "Money-in-Politics Stories Driving the News in 2023," Open Secrets, December 21, 2023.
24. Heidi Przybyla, "Leonard Leo Used Federalist Society Contact to Obtain $1.6 Billion Donation," Politico, May 2, 2023.
25. Andrew Perez, "GOP Puppetmaster Expands His Dark-Money Operation," *Rolling Stone*, November 9, 2023.

26. Joshua Kaplan, Justin Elliott, and Alex Mierjeski, "Clarence Thomas and the Billionaire," ProPublica, April 6, 2023.
27. John McCain was the last major party presidential candidate to run using the federal public financing system. See Julia Cage, "How Barack Obama Spurred the End of America's Public Presidential Election Funding System," ProMarket, April 27, 2020.
28. Massoglia, "Money-in-Politics Stories."
29. See "Annotated Guide to the For the People Act of 2021," Brennan Center, March 18, 2021, www.brennancenter.org/our-work/policy-solutions/annotated-guide-people-act-2021.
30. Ashley Archibald and Lisa Edge, "Vying for Votes: Interview with City Council District 6 Candidate Dan Strauss," *Real Change,* October 2, 2019.

10. FOUR OTHER WAYS THE BILLIONAIRES ARE MESSING WITH YOUR LIFE

1. "Employment Projections, Employment by Major Industry Sector," table 2.1, U.S. Bureau of Labor Statistics, 2022, www.bls.gov/bdm/nonprofits/nonprofits.htm.
2. In 2022, Amazon founder Jeff Bezos, for instance, told CNN that he would be giving away most of his fortune in his lifetime. Brian Fung, "Exclusive: Jeff Bezos Says He Will Give Most of His Money to Charity," CNN Business, November 14, 2022. In 2015, Meta founder and CEO Mark Zuckerberg announced he would give away what he makes from 99 percent of his Facebook shares. Heather Kelly, "Zuckerberg Pledges 99% of Facebook Stock to Charitable Causes," CNN Business, December 2, 2015.
3. "Frequently Asked Questions," Giving Pledge, givingpledge.org/faq.
4. Some of this drop is a decline in the market value of Scott's assets, which started at $36 billion after her divorce from Jeff Bezos. Sophie Alexander, "MacKenzie Scott Renews Giving After Unloading $8 Billion of Stock," Bloomberg, November 14, 2024.

5. Feeney, who gave away nearly all his fortune, was the inspiration for the Giving Pledge. He wrote a booklet called "Zero Is the Hero" about his experience giving away $9 billion through Atlantic Philanthropies, www.atlanticphilanthropies.org/insights/insights-books/zero-is-the-hero.
6. Chuck Collins, Helen Flannery, Omar Ocampo, and Kalena Thomhave, "The Giving Pledge at 10: A Case Study in Top Heavy Philanthropy," Institute for Policy Studies, August 2020.
7. Musk appeared on the Forbes billionaire list in 2012 with $2 billion. As of January 1, 2025, Musk was worth $428.82 billion, www.forbes.com/profile/elon-musk/?list=rtb.
8. Michael Mechanic, "Those 'Giving Pledge' Billionaires Had Better Pick Up the Pace," *Mother Jones,* November 28, 2023.
9. Helen Flannery, "Donor-Advised Funds Now Consume a Quarter of Individual Charitable Giving," Inequality.org, December 22, 2023.
10. Chuck Collins and Helen Flannery, "Gilded Giving 2022: How Wealth Inequality Distorts Philanthropy and Imperils Democracy," Institute for Policy Studies, July 2022.
11. Chuck Collins, Bella DeVaan, and Helen Flannery, "Gilded Giving 2024: Saving Philanthropy from Wall Street," Institute for Policy Studies, December 5, 2024. Also see Ray D. Madoff, "5 Myths About Payout Rules for Donor-Advised Funds," *Chronicle of Philanthropy,* January 13, 2014.
12. Chuck Collins and Helen Flannery, "Top Heavy Philanthropy in 8 Charts," Inequality.org, March 3, 2022.
13. Whit Hunter, "What Is the 80/20 Rule in Fundraising?" Betterworld, August 2024, betterworld.org/blog/fundraising/80-20-fundraising-rule.
14. "Charitable Contribution Deductions," Internal Revenue Service, August 27, 2024, www.irs.gov/charities-non-profits/charitable-organizations/charitable-contribution-deductions.
15. Mike Scutari, "It Isn't Good News: Trump's Tax Law Caused a $16 Billion Annual Decrease in Charitable Giving," *Inside Philanthropy,* August 20, 2024.

16. Chuck Collins, "For Every Buck a Billionaire Gives to Charity, You Chip in Up to 74 Cents," Inequality.org, March 19, 2021.
17. Collins and Flannery, "Gilded Giving 2022."
18. Maria Di Mento and Carmen Mendoza, "2023's Top Donors: Where They Live, Where They Give, and More," *Chronicle of Philanthropy*, March 5, 2024.
19. Di Mento and Mendoza.
20. Helen Flannery and Brian Mittendorf, "Charitable Objectives or Donor Benefits? What Sponsor Language Reveals About Donor-Advised Fund Priorities and Resource Flows," August 9, 2024, ssrn .com/abstract=4565216.
21. Chuck Collins and Helen Flannery, "Tax Rules, Investment Houses, and Donor-Advised Funds: What's at Stake?" *Nonprofit Quarterly*, April 3, 2024.
22. Helen Flannery and Bella DeVaan, "What Could Our Working Charities Do with $339 Billion? Let's Find Out," Inequality.org, August 8, 2024.
23. See the Donor Revolt at www.donorrevolt.com.
24. Austin Frerick, *Barons: Money, Power, and the Corruption of America's Food Industry* (Washington, DC: Island Press, 2024), 172.
25. Jamie Konopacky and Soren Rundquist, "EWG Study and Mapping Show Large CAFOs in Iowa Up Fivefold Since 1990," Environmental Working Group, January 21, 2020, www.ewg.org/interactive-maps /2020-iowa-cafos.
26. Ron Knox, "State Attorney General—Fighting Monopoly Power," Institute for Local Self Reliance, July 2020.
27. Andrea Murphy, "America's Largest Private Companies," *Forbes*, November 14, 2023. Also see Frerick, *Barons*, 31.
28. "Profile: Cargill-MacMillan Family," *Forbes* Real Time Billionaires List, www.forbes.com/profile/cargill-macmillan-1/?sh=33f54bf23b6c. The family's net worth was $60.6 billion as of November 2024.
29. Oliver Bullough, "The Great American Tax Haven: Why the Super-Rich Love South Dakota," *The Guardian*, November 14, 2019.
30. Frerick, *Barons*, 43–44.

31. Hidemi Hattori, Yuma Hanai, Yuto Oshima, Hiroaki Kataoka, and Nozomu Eto, "Excessive Intake of High-Fructose Corn Syrup Drinks Induces Impaired Glucose Tolerance," *Biomedicines* 9, no. 5 (2021): 541, doi.org/10.3390/biomedicines9050541.
32. "Profile: Wolfgang Reimann," *Forbes* Real Time Billionaires List, www.forbes.com/profile/wolfgang-reimann/?sh=7910ca537a73.
33. Frerick, *Barons*, 57.
34. "Farmworkers Who Picked Driscoll's Strawberries in Oxnard File Suit Alleging Stolen Wages," California Rural Legal Assistance, April 17, 2023, crla.org/articles/farmworkers-who-picked-driscolls-strawberries-oxnard-file-suit-alleging-stolen-wages.
35. Frerick, *Barons*, 118.
36. Chuck Collins, "801 Billionaires Hold a Combined $6.2 Trillion in Wealth," Inequality.org, September 17, 2024. See "Profile: Walton Family," *Forbes* Real Time Billionaires List, www.forbes.com/profile/walton-1/?sh=1469587a6f3f.
37. States were the origin of antitrust and anti-monopoly law, but many have yielded that power to the federal government. Ron Knox, "Fighting Monopoly Power: State Attorneys General," Institute for Local Self Reliance, July 2020.
38. Frerick, *Barons*, 172.
39. Katie Thomas, "The Costs of Caring for Pets," *New York Times,* June 23, 2024.
40. H.O. Taylor, T.K. Cudjoe, F. Bu, et al., "The State of Loneliness and Social Isolation Research: Current Knowledge and Future Directions," *BMC Public Health* 23, no. 1049 (2023).
41. Stephen J. Dubner, "Do You Know Who Owns Your Vet?" *Freakonomics Radio,* episode 532, January 25, 2023.
42. Ross Kelly, "Pandemic Hastens Ongoing Trend in Veterinary Consolidation," *VinNews*, December 30, 2021.
43. Ed Boks, "Navigating the Rising Costs of Veterinary Care: A Call to Action for Animal Welfare Organizations," *Animal Politics with Ed Boks* (blog), July 8, 2024, animalpolitics.substack.com/p/the-high-cost-of-compassion-navigating.

44. "Profile: Mars Family," *Forbes* Real Time Billionaires List, December 31, 2024, www.forbes.com/profile/mars-1.
45. See more at Mars Petcare: www.mars.com/our-brands/petcare.
46. The Reimanns were also known as unbridled antisemites and early and enthusiastic supporters of Adolf Hitler. See Katrin Bennhold, "Germany's Second-Richest Family Discovers a Dark Nazi Past," *New York Times,* March 25, 2019.
47. John R. Fischer, "Vet Care Sees Strong PE Demand: 4 Deals Announced in 2024, with More to Come," PE Hub, June 21, 2024.
48. Stephen J. Dubner, "Should You Trust Private Equity to Take Care of Your Dog?" *Freakonomics Radio,* episode 531, January 18, 2023.
49. Kay O'Rourke, correspondence with the author, July 14, 2024. See the nineteen-page "Terms of Service" to get the full picture: www.rover.com/terms/tos.
50. "Rover Agrees to be Acquired by Blackstone in $2.3 Billion Transaction," press release, Rover, www.rover.com/blog/press-release/rover-agrees-to-be-acquired-by-blackstone-in-2-3-billion-transaction.
51. Prison Policy Initiative, "Prisoners in 2022," September 2023, www.prisonpolicy.org/blog/2020/01/16/percent-incarcerated.
52. Derek Seidman, "Private Equity Is Using Prison Phone, Food and Health System to Rack Up Profits," Truthout, November 24, 2023.
53. "Profile: Tom Gores," *Forbes* Real Time Billionaires List, www.forbes.com/profile/tom-gores.
54. Seidman, "Private Equity."
55. Kalena Thomhave, "California's Legislature Made Prison Phone Calls Free—Utility Regulators Can Handle the Rest," *American Prospect,* May 8, 2023.

11. DISRUPTING THE NARRATIVES THAT JUSTIFY BILLIONAIRE WEALTH

1. The GDP of Denmark in 2023 was $395 billion. "GDP by Country," Worldometer, www.worldometers.info/gdp/gdp-by-country.

2. "Americans and Billionaires Survey," Harris Poll Thought Leadership Practice, wave 2, August 2024, theharrispoll.com/wp-content/uploads/2024/07/Americans-and-Billionaires-Survey-August-2024.pdf.
3. Ben Cohen and Jerry Greenfield, "We Don't Need This Stupid Tax Cut," *USA Today,* April 16, 2015.

12. AN AGENDA TO REDUCE BILLIONAIRE POWER AND IMPROVE OUR LIVES

1. Ingrid Robeyns, "Limitarianism: Why We Need to Put a Cap on the Super-Rich," *The Guardian,* January 21, 2024.
2. See Chuck Collins, *Is Inequality in America Irreversible?* (London: Polity Books, 2018).
3. "CPI Inflation Calculator," Bureau of Labor Statistics, data.bls.gov/cgi-bin/cpicalc.pl?cost1=7.25&year1=200907&year2=202409.
4. Jeanna Smialek, "Waitresses Stuck at $2.13 Hourly Minimum for 22 Years," *Businessweek,* April 23, 2013. Also see "State Minimum Wages" National Conference of State Legislatures,. www.ncsl.org/labor-and-employment/state-minimum-wages.
5. Jennifer Tolbert, Rakesh Singh, and Patrick Drake, "The Uninsured Population and Health Coverage," Kaiser Family Foundation, May 28, 2024, www.kff.org/health-policy-101-the-uninsured-population-and-health-coverage/?entry=table-of-contents-introduction.
6. Christine Emba, "Universal Basic Income," *Washington Post,* September 28, 2015.
7. Ashifa Kassam, "Ontario Plans to Launch Universal Basic Income Trial Run This Summer," *The Guardian,* April 24, 2017.
8. Justin Schweitzer, Emily DiMatteo, and Nick Buffie, "How Dehumanizing Administrative Burdens Harm Disabled People," Center for American Progress, December 5, 2022.
9. Richard Freeman, ed., *Working Under Different Rules* (New York: Russell Sage Foundation, 1994).

10. Michael Findley, Daniel L. Nielson, and Jason Sharman, *Global Shell Games: Experiments in Transnational Relations, Crime, and Terrorism* (Cambridge: Cambridge University Press, 2014). See also Global Shell Games, www.globalshellgames.com.
11. See Bill Gates Sr. and Chuck Collins, *Wealth and Our Commonwealth: Why America Should Tax Accumulated Fortunes* (Boston: Beacon Press, 2003).
12. Jason Ma, "Billionaires vs. Millionaires: America's Wealthy Are More Eager Than Janet Yellen to Tax the Super-Wealthy," *Fortune,* June 23, 2024.
13. Tim Wu, *The Curse of Bigness: Antitrust in the New Gilded Age* (New York: Columbia Global Reports, 2018).
14. See Barry Lynn, *Cornered: The New Monopoly Capitalism and the Economics of Destruction* (Hoboken, NJ: Wiley, 2010).
15. David Dayen, "Look to the State Trustbusters," *American Prospect,* November 15, 2024.
16. See a summary of policies to reduce excessive CEO pay, including the Tax Excessive CEO Pay Act, at "Executive Excess 2024," Institute for Policy Studies, August 2024. https://ips-dc.org/report-executive-excess-2024/.
17. "Americans and Billionaires Survey."
18. See the National Center for Employee Ownership, "What the Research Says: The Impact of Employee Ownership." www.nceo.org/research/research-findings-on-employee-ownership.
19. *CDFI 20th Anniversary Report,* CDFI Coalition, March 5, 2014, www.cdfi.org/cdfi-20th-anniversary-report. See the 2019 report here: cdfi.org/2019-report.
20. Aaron Klein, "What Is a Financial Transaction Tax?" Brookings Institution, March 27, 2020. https://www.brookings.edu/articles/what-is-a-financial-transaction-tax-2.
21. For more information on B Corporations, see the B Lab website, www.bcorporation.net. Today, more than two thousand certified B Corps from fifty countries and more than 130 industries work together to redefine success in business. Businesses are evaluated

and scored on wages, working conditions (such as family leave, stock options for employees, and flexible hours), environmental practices, community involvement, procurement practices, energy use, and waste management, as well as other criteria.

22. See Bill Gates Sr. and Chuck Collins, "A GI Bill for the Next Generation," *Houston Chronicle,* June 22, 2004.
23. Chris Hayes, "MSNBC Town Hall with Bernie Sanders," MSNBC, April 25, 2016.
24. For information on the Alaska Permanent Fund, see "United States," International Forum of Sovereign Wealth Funds, www.ifswf.org /members/usa.
25. See "Cap 'n Dividend," video, 1:50, posted December 16, 2008, by PeterBarnesTV, www.youtube.com/watch?v=moj_0rGFxRQ.
26. For information about the legislation, see the Cap & Dividend website, climateandprosperity.org. For the details of the "Healthy Climate" bill, see "The Bill," Cap & Dividend, climateandprosperity .org/the-bill.

CONCLUSION

1. Peter Turchin, "The Deep Historical Forces That Explain Trump's Win," *The Guardian,* November 30, 2024.
2. Oliver Balch, "The Relevance of Gandhi in the Capitalism Debate," *The Guardian,* January 28, 2013.
3. Lydia Saad, "More in U.S. See Unions Strengthening and Want It That Way," Gallup, August 30, 2023, news.gallup.com/poll/510281 /unions-strengthening.aspx.
4. William Diep, "Voters Strongly Support a Billionaire Minimum Tax," Data for Progress, September 12, 2024, www.dataforprogress .org/blog/2024/9/12/voters-strongly-support-a-billionaire-minimum -tax.
5. Rob Todaro and Anika Dandekar, "Much of the Congressional Progressive Caucus' New Legislative Agenda Is Popular with Swing

Voters," Data for Progress, April 29, 2024, www.dataforprogress.org/blog/2024/4/29/much-of-congressional-progressive-caucus-agenda-popular-with-swing-state-voters.

6. "Americans and Billionaires Survey," Harris Poll Thought Leadership Practice, wave 2, August 2024, theharrispoll.com/wp-content/uploads/2024/07/Americans-and-Billionaires-Survey-August-2024.pdf.
7. See the Patriotic Millionaires website, www.patrioticmillionaires.org.
8. See Chuck Collins, "Helping the Rich Let Go," *Yes!* August 10, 2021.
9. Aisha Alli, "Inside the Secret Society of 'Progressive' Wealth Advisors," *Spears*, April 28, 2023.
10. Evan Osnos, "The Getty Family's Trust Issues," *New Yorker*, January 16, 2023.
11. Justine Epstein, "Surrendering Wealth," *Kosmos* 24, no. 3, 2024.
12. Check out sources such as Common Dreams, ProPublica, Truthout, and the Intercept, among others.

ILLUSTRATION CREDITS

25 www.cartoonstock.com

29 Institute for Policy Studies (www.inequality.org/facts/burned-by-billionaires)

31 Institute for Policy Studies (www.inequality.org/facts/burned-by-billionaires)

32 Institute for Policy Studies (www.inequality.org/facts/burned-by-billionaires)

49 Economic Policy Institute, "The Productivity Pay Gap"

50 U.S. Census Bureau, "Current Population Survey"

51 Emmanuel Saez, "Striking it Richer: The Evolution of Top Incomes in the United States"

52 *Forbes*'s Real-Time Billionaires List

53 Louis Federal Reserve

55 U.S. Federal Reserve

63 Richard Wilk and Beatrix Barros, *The Conversation*

69 www.cartoonstock.com

71 "The State of Yachting," *Superyacht Times* (March 26, 2024)

73 Instagram

80 www.cartoonstock.com

91 Institute on Taxation and Economic Policy, "Who Pays?" (2024)

93 www.cartoonstock.com

95 www.cartoonstock.com

107 *Private Equity International* and *Forbes*'s Real-Time Billionaires List

111 www.cartoonstock.com

137 www.cartoonstock.com

154 www.cartoonstock.com

186 www.cartoonstock.com

All graphs available at www.inequality.org/facts/burned-by-billionaires.

ABOUT THE AUTHOR

Chuck Collins is a senior scholar at the Institute for Policy Studies where he coedits Inequality.org. He is the author of several books including *Born on Third Base, The Wealth Hoarders,* and, with Bill Gates Sr., *Wealth and Our Commonwealth*. He lives in Vermont.

www.ingramcontent.com/pod-product-compliance
Lightning Source LLC
Chambersburg PA
CBHW051722260326
41914CB00031B/1693/J

* 9 7 8 1 6 2 0 9 7 9 0 9 9 *